SEW SIMPLY, SEW RIGHT

SEW SIMPLY, SEW RIGHT

by

Mini Rhea
and
Frances S. Leighton

AVENEL BOOKS • NEW YORK

Illustrations by Bonnie Sue Kaplan

517104172
Copyright © MCMLXIX by Fleet Press Corporation.
Library of Congress Catalog Card Number: 72-76031
All rights reserved.
No part of this book may be reproduced or utilized in any form
or by any means, electronic or mechanical, including photocopying,
recording, or by any information storage and retrieval system,
without permission in writing from the publisher.
Inquiries should be addressed to:
Avenel Books,
a division of
Crown Publishers, Inc.,
419 Park Avenue South
New York, New York, 10016.
This edition is published by Avenel Books,
a division of Crown Publishers, Inc.
by arrangement with Fleet Press Corporation.
abcdefgh
Manufactured in the United States of America.

INTRODUCTION

You are about to embark on a great adventure. The joy of sewing will be yours if you learn to sew so easily that you can enjoy the exciting results of your labor the same day you start your project.

If you follow the easy instructions in this book, you will soon be able to sew a whole dress within a few hours, and what is more, the way it fits will be the envy of your friends. Furthermore, each dress will be unique, created just for you. In this day of packaged products, sewing is one of the few remaining forms of self expression left for women to gain fulfilment in creating beauty for themselves and their families.

This book is for beginners. But it is also for those who have tried sewing but are unhappy because their clothes have that "homemade" look. Do not fear. If you are a willing student who truly follows the step by step instructions in this easy-to-use book, you will achieve the professional look which sets every well dressed woman apart from the crowd. You can achieve the look of high fashion and quality while saving hundreds of dollars for yourself and your family.

This book is actually the complete primer for everyone, the simplified guide for sewing. It will teach you how to make a garment step by step from the pattern you have selected. It will show you how to adjust the pattern to your own individual requirements. You will learn the inside secrets of a perfect construction just as if you had learned it all in a custom workroom. You will even have help in picking patterns that make the most of your good points and minimize the bad.

If you have ready-made garments in your closet which you will not wear because they do not fit right, this book will show you how to alter them.

Even if you have never held a needle in your hand before, you should, after reading this book, go about the making of your first dress with confidence. The author spent twenty-one years in learning all the things contained in it and has sewn for many of the most famous people in the political and social worlds.

Today, with thousands of dresses behind me, and more thousands of people wearing clothes that have been designed by me, I feel fully confident that I can help you turn out professional looking clothes, even if you have never held a needle in your hand before. I recall that in 1947 when that first sign went up, "MINI RHEA, DRESSMAKER," I faced an immediate crisis. For, as my shingle went up the skirts went down with a crash from knee length to ankle length—the New Look, they called it.

Women came to me in desperation saying, "I'm ruined. I just bought these dresses; I just bought these suits. I can't afford more. What can I do with them?" I found myself putting yokes on skirts, inserting strips of contrasting colors at various places in dresses to create interesting effects while at the same time lengthening the skirts. I also made ruffles and flounces if the design and material were suitable. I had no choice but to use my imagination, and it was given a thorough workout.

At the insistence of my customers I moved to Georgetown. where again fate overtook me. One of my customers in Georgetown was Jacqueline Bouvier who was brought in by another customer, her mother, Mrs. Hugh Auchincloss. We grew to be good friends.

I watched Jacqueline develop her style sense and learned much from her. The look which she developed before my eyes became the rage of the world when, in 1960, her husband became the President of the United States. That was the first time a publisher asked for my experiences. You may have read the story, "I Was Jacqueline Kennedy's Dressmaker." In the book I told about Jackie the career girl, who came flying in breathlessly with an armload of fashion magazines, full of ideas for her next creation, and how, when young Congressman Kennedy was courting her, she used my place as a second home to relax in or to effect a quick change when she didn't have time to go home.

About the time the book was published I opened a custom salon in Philadelphia. I also started traveling from coast to coast conducting fashion clinics where I taught women what they should know about clothes, how to choose their wardrobes, and how to dress to bring out their own individuality.

In 1966, while still conducting fashion clinics, I became a designer for the Minnesota Woolen Company which now is my major activity. I'm back in Washington now and spend my spare time between designing two lines a year, traveling around the country, appearing on TV, and lecturing on fashion.

I hope that you will enjoy this book as well as benefit from it. I would be happy to hear how you enjoy sewing after trying it my way.

Mini Rhea

CONTENTS

SEW SIMPLY, SEW RIGHT

CHAPTER 1

EQUIP YOURSELF FOR ACTION

All the Things You Will Need and Why

Sewing Box: If you don't want to buy a fancy sewing box, any strong box 9 inches or 10 inches by 15 inches or 16 inches will be fine for holding all your sewing equipment as well as your patterns. Rule number 1 is to keep organized so that everything you need is always at your finger tips.

A Tape measure: Use a cloth one with metal clips over the ends.

A Thimble: Thimbles have not gone out of fashion. For rapid sewing, you need one to protect your middle finger when pushing a needle through, otherwise your sewing is slow and halting. Choose one that fits snugly enough not to fall off.

A Metal Slide Gauge: This is very handy for measuring hems and making sure that the depth of the hem is the same all the way around.

4 or 6 Inch Scissors: For cutting thread and trimming seams.

7 or 8 Inch Cutting Shears: Used for cutting out patterns or cutting material of any considerable size.

Pinking Shears: You will need them for finishing off seams that would ravel. Never use them for cutting out garments. Seven inch shears are comfortable for pinking.

Needles: Get a package of assorted sizes. You will want to use a larger one for basting or sewing on buttons, and smaller, thinner ones for hemming and hand finishing. A long eye is easier to thread than a small round eye.

A Box of Pins: Get silk pins because they are rustproof and thinner so that they don't leave pin marks in the fabric. Also, a sewing machine with hinged pressure foot sews right over these pins when they are placed across the line you are stitching.

11

Slide gauge for measuring hems and short distances

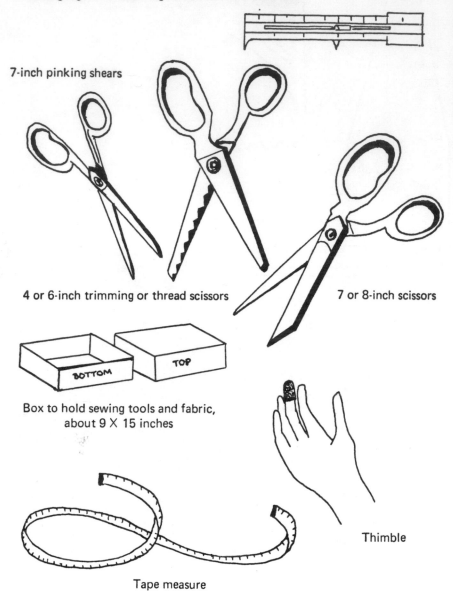

7-inch pinking shears

4 or 6-inch trimming or thread scissors

7 or 8-inch scissors

BOTTOM

TOP

Box to hold sewing tools and fabric,
about 9 X 15 inches

Thimble

Tape measure

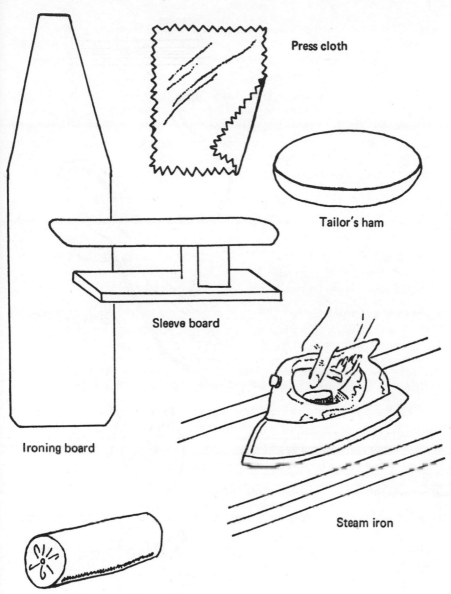

Press cloth

Tailor's ham

Sleeve board

Ironing board

Steam iron

Seam roll

13

Pin Cushion: You can keep your assortment of most-used needles on it, as well as have a place to put your pins as you use them. A wrist pin cushion is best since you would always have them handy.

Thread: Black and white thread should always be in your sewing kit even if you don't wear those colors. They are perfect for basting your material in a contrasting color, so the stitches are easy to find when you are taking them out. Mercerized thread is used for almost all sewing. The only time you will need different thread is when you are working on wool jersey, dacron or nylon. In those cases use dacron or nymo thread, which is a single filament nylon thread. Be sure to match your thread to each garment you make. Take a little sample of the cloth with you when shopping for it.

Tracing Wheel: This is used with tracing paper to mark your fabric with the pattern marking such as darts, seam lines and buttonholes.

Dressmaker's Tracing Paper: This is a paper which is similar to carbon paper and is used with the tracing wheel to transfer pattern markings to the fabric. It comes in various colors.

Dressmaker's Transparent Ruler: This is a must for marking straight lines with your tracing wheel, as well as for many occasions when you need to measure while seeing underneath.

Tailor's Chalk: Get several colors. This is used to mark the wrong sides of fabric and to show the various pattern alterations.

All the preceding things will be kept in your sewing box when not in use. The following are also part of your equipment.

Yardstick: For measuring the length of your skirt hems. Also available is a standing hem marker, though this is a little more expensive.

Sewing Machine:

1. Adjustable zipper foot-this helps you stitch close to the edge of the zipper on either side.
2. Seam guide-this is great for making straight seams the precise width indicated on the pattern and is adjustable for various widths of seams.

All stores that sell sewing machines give instructions in their use. If your machine has been in the family for some time, a store selling that particular make will be glad to show you how to use it.

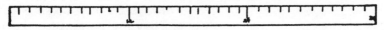
Yardstick

Wrist pincushion

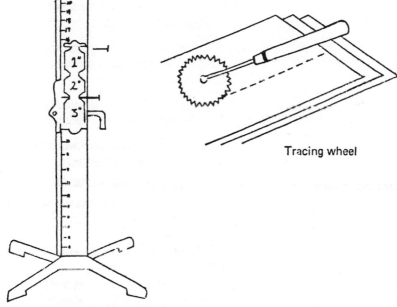
Tracing wheel

Hem marker

Pressing Equipment: Besides a regular ironing board you will need the following to do really professional, quality sewing.

1. Sleeve Board—this is not only good for sleeves, but for pressing small areas of the garment as you work on them.
2. Pressing Cushions—get a seam roll or a ham shaped cushion. Used for pressing curved or shaped areas, such as shoulder lines and sleeve caps.
3. Steam Iron—it is a good investment and should be used to press open each seam as you sew. This is the true secret of giving your sewing a professional look.
4. Press Cloths—a heavyweight cloth is recommended for pressing woolens and a lighter weight for pressing silks and synthetic fabrics.

CHAPTER 2

PICKING YOUR PATTERN
Pattern Language—Finding Your Figure Type—Illusion of Line

Since we are talking mainly to the beginner, we would suggest that you select a simple pattern to start with. We are shortly going to explain exactly how to make a simple dress—a shift or sheath. After that you can go on to the chapter which tells you how to make a two piece dress or a skirt and blouse.

The best kinds of patterns for a beginner are those that have few pieces and are plainly marked with directions. At the end of this chapter we will give a list of pattern terminology to enable you to read your pattern as easily as you read your newspaper.

The beginner should stay away from shirtwaists—dresses or blouses—complicated collars, bias cut dresses and suits or coats. Leave these until you have gotten the feel of sewing one or two simple dresses and feel completely at home with the sewing machine.

WHAT FIGURE TYPE ARE YOU?

Before you buy your first pattern, you must determine your figure type because patterns are cut with a particular figure in mind. There are several basic figure types.

Misses': More of this type pattern is sold than any other. Misses' patterns are for the average type figure and run in sizes from 10 to 20.

Women's: These patterns are proportionately larger than the Misses' and run from size 40 to 44. But this does not mean bust size, since a size 40 women's pattern is for a woman with a size 42 bust, 34 waist and 44 hip.

Junior Miss or Junior: These are for the more slender, and smaller waisted figure. The Junior designation has nothing to do with age. These patterns are given in odd numbers, 9 to 15.

17

Junior Petite: The Junior Petite pattern is for the shorter junior type figure, the girl or woman about 5'1", with a small waist line and full hips. Sizes run from 3JP to 13JP.

Teen: These patterns are for the teenager and are designed with appropriate youthful styling. They run from size 10 T to 16 T for growing girls with bust 30 to 36.

Half Sizes: Half sizes are fuller junior sizes and run from 12½ to 24½. They are for the mature woman who has a little fuller than average bust, waist and hip measurement as well as being short waisted. In general, the half sizer's shoulders are narrower than average.

Different pattern companies have a slight variation in their sizes, especially in the Junior and Petite designations. Do not panic, as long as you have your own body measurements you will have no trouble finding the pattern closest to your size.

HOW TO DETERMINE YOUR OWN BASIC BODY TYPE

To prepare for measuring, first of all put on the same foundation garments you will be wearing under the dress you are about to make. Also, be sure to wear a thin garment over the foundation garment so there will be no bulkiness of cloth. In taking the measurements the tape should be held close but not tight enough to indent the figure. It would be helpful to have a friend do the measuring for you.

Bust: Bring tape straight across the back and over the fullest part of the bust.

Waist: Take the measurement at the narrowest part of the waist.

Hip: Measure down seven inches from your natural waistline, and draw the tape around your hips at this point.

Back of Neck Base to Natural Waistline: This is the measurement which determines if you are shortwaisted. Measure from the base of the back of the neck down to your waistline.

18

Teen   **Junior**   **Junior Petite**

Misses'   **Half-Size**   **Women's**

To see where you belong look at the chart below:

MISSES' SIZES

Size	10	12	14	16	18	20
Bust	31	32	34	36	38	40
Waist	24	25	26	28	30	32
Hip	33	34	36	38	40	42
Back Waist Length	15¾	16	16¼	16½	16¾	17

WOMEN'S SIZES

Size	40	42	44
Bust	42	44	46
Waist	34	36	38½
Hip	44	46	48
Back Waist Length	17⅛	17¼	17⅜

HALF SIZES

Size	12½	14½	16½	18½	20½	22½	24½
Bust	33	35	37	39	41	43	45
Waist	27	29	31	33	35	37½	40
Hip	37	39	41	43	45	47	49
Back Waist Length	15¼	15½	15¾	16	16¼	16½	16¾

JUNIOR MISS OR JUNIOR SIZES

Size	9	11	13	15
Bust	30½	31½	33	35
Waist	23½	24½	25½	27
Hip	32½	33½	35	37
Back Waist Length	15	15¼	15½	15¾

TEEN SIZES

Size	10T	12T	14T	16T
Bust	30	32	34	36
Waist	24	25	26	28
Hip	32	34	36	38
Back Waist Length	14¾	15	15¼	15½

JUNIOR PETITE SIZES

Size	3JP	5JP	7JP	9JP	11JP	13JP
Bust	31	31½	32	32½	33	33½
Waist	22½	23	23½	24	24½	25
Hip	32½	33	33½	34	34½	35
Back Waist Length	14	14¼	14½	14¾	15	15¼

20

Now you know your basic type. The next step is to select a pattern whose lines will do the most for you. You can also give illusions with colors and types of fabrics, but these two areas are so important that we will take them up in a separate chapter, "All About Fabrics and How to Choose Your Own."

THE ILLUSION OF LINE

It is amazing how much the lines of a garment can do for you. But optical illusions are no mystery; they are carefully constructed to make the viewer's eyes focus where you want them to. If you want to focus attention on your legs, for example, a ruffle or contrasting edging around the bottom of a dress will do just that.

If you would like to look slimmer, look for a pattern that has a straight line from neck to hem, perhaps in the form of a strip of contrasting color, or a line of buttons from neck to hem, and you will do just that.

Slim skirt for slimmer look; bouffant skirt for heavier look

A ruffle or contrasting edging to focus attention
on legs

If you have a lovely neck, show it off; don't hide it with a lot of bulky collars. Leave it bare. Just because a pattern comes with a collar doesn't mean you have to use it.

Everyone can wear either a shift or a sheath, such as we are going to make in the chapter "How to Make a Dress the Easy Way." These are both one-piece dresses. The difference between the two is that the shift hangs loose while the sheath has darts both front and back to give it a more fitted look. Also the side seams of the sheath are slightly shaped.

For those who need to wear something at the neck these dresses are the perfect background for scarves, jewelry, or detachable collars.

The slim person can wear the shift or the sheath, but the person with fuller hips or larger bust will find she will look better in a fitted sheath because otherwise she will look as heavy all over as the widest part of her.

To Look Taller or Slimmer — Concentrate on vertical lines to keep the eye moving upward. A plain sheath will do this. So will a coat dress with V neckline and a shirt waist dress with a single row of buttons down the front.

Avoid belts and anything which makes the eye travel horizontally, also avoid dresses in which the skirt and the top are of different colors. Avoid much trimming or detail. Avoid strapless dresses.

22

For shorter and more full-figured look

To Look Shorter and More Full Figured — Stress horizontal lines including belts and dropped waistlines with gathered skirts.

Yokes at the bustline are also good. So are double-breasted dresses. Go in for full skirts, A-line, flared or pleated. Square necklines will make you look shorter, also the bateau or straight across neckline.

One good trick is to use two colors, either a skirt or yoke of contrasting color to the rest of the dress.

Capes tend to reduce height but may be worn by a short person if they are not too bulky and are of the right proportion.

Details are eyecatching and make a person look heavier and shorter—impressive collars, shirring, scarves, soft bows and outstanding lapels. Wide loose sleeves also cut size and make you look heavier.

Avoid narrow skirts, vertical lines, and dresses which hug the figure too closely.

For taller or slimmer look

TO HIDE FIGURE FAULTS

For Flabby or Heavy Upper Arms: You should always wear sleeves. For evening gowns wear stoles over the shoulders, or a floating chiffon panel attached at the shoulders. For daytime wear sleeves that are not too tight over the upper arm. A raglan sleeve is very comfortable for the person with a heavy upper arm.

For Long Thin Arms: Wear dolman sleeves. Wear wide full sleeves. Wear wide cuffs at the wrist.

For Square Shoulders: Wear raglan sleeves or draw attention away from them with large collars or lapels, especially of contrasting color.

For Narrow or Sloping Shoulders: You may need to build up the shoulder with shoulder pads. Also a lapel that is set high on the shoulder and is stiffened to stand a little away from the shoulder gives the effect of width.

For Long Thin Neck: Wear lots of turtle necks of bulky material, also Peter Pan collars and Chinese necklines. Also wear scarves.

For Short Neck: The more area of skin you show around the neck the more you give the illusion of a longer neck. Wear V-necks or a low soft cowl neckline. If your pattern has a jewel neckline, you can cut the curve a little deeper in the neckline. A square neckline may also be used.

For Small Bust: Don't hesitate to wear padded bras. Also curved lines over the bust gives the illusion of a larger bust. To achieve this, wear patch pockets with the lower part curved. Also you can find patterns with a yoke that has shirring right at the bustline. For dressier occasions a big bow of stiff or bulky material worn center front will help the illusion.

For Large Bust: Avoid like the plague a tight fit across the bust. Your bodice should always have a looseness or ease. A crossed wrap around bodice that forms a diagonal line across the bust is very good. Darts at the shoulder line that release fullness across the bust are good. A wide panel of another color down the center front slims the bustline and the whole overall look.

For a Roll of Fat Above the Waistline: The loose overblouse is made for you. Never wear close fitting waistlines, but if you do have a waistline seam, always have gathers or darts that release fullness above the waist to camouflage the roll.

For Protruding Stomach: Never let the skirt dip in under the stomach. Wear skirts with a slight fullness. A-line skirts are good, so are soft gathers falling from the waist all across the front of the skirt. Also, you can wear finger tip length overblouses or jackets.

For Large Hips: Draw attention to shoulders and necklines, thus drawing the eye away from this figure fault. Use only skirts which are loose and easy, never tight and narrow. Use A-line or gored skirts.

For Narrow Hips: Gathered skirts are very good or a long torso with gathers released at the hipline. Pleats can be used in the same way. Bulky pockets may be placed at various places. When far to the side and stiffened to stand ajar, they give the effect of wider hips.

With these rules in mind you should have no trouble in finding the pattern that does the most for your figure.

Styles may come and styles may go, but these rules are basic and can be applied regardless of the whims of fashion.

There is one more thing which you should consider before picking your pattern; that is your facial type. There is beauty in every type face—the heart shaped face, the oval, square, the round, and the oblong face. But it is true that particular lines at the neck enhance the beauty of each type. So take a look in the mirror, and see if your face is longer than average (oblong), square at the chin line, pointed, or heart shaped in the chin line, round and wide at the cheek bones or perfectly oval. Then check below to see the best neckline for your facial contour:

NECKLINES

For Oval Face: You are a lucky one who can wear any neckline unless you have some other problem such as a neck that is too long and thin.

For Round Face: Avoid lines that repeat the roundness of your face. Wear V-necks and square necks and any neckline that has angles in it.

For Oblong Face: To make a long face look rounder wear high necklines. Wear lots of collars, especially those that come high under your chin, or have some little attention getter like an edging or a button or jewelry at the neckline if there is no collar. Bateau necklines are also good for you as well as lapels that add width.

26

For Square Face: You can cut the square effect of the jawline by choosing necklines which have depth such as deep V's and deep ovals even if you then have to fill it in with either jewelry or a little bib of contrasting color. A deep cowl neckline is also good.

For the Heart Shaped Face: To counteract a pointed chin you can wear every shaped neckline that adds width such as square necklines or sweetheart necklines. Like a longer faced girl, you can also wear bateau neck. The jewel neckline is perfect for you.

Oval

Oblong

Round

Heart

Square

PATTERN TALK

You have now opened your pattern, and are probably completely confused from all the pieces that you see. But do not be dismayed, for it is really very simple and will all become clear as you look at each piece. You did not know there would be so many pieces. Probably you won't need them all.

The different styles are called "View A, B, or C, etc." or "View 1, 2, 3, etc."

There are usually several variations in each pattern—sometimes to give different collar effects, sometimes various skirts, and sometimes adding a coat or jacket.

The first thing you will want to do is take the instruction guide out of the pattern envelope and find the cutting layout for the style of the garment you are going to make.

Draw a circle around this cutting guide so you will not become confused when you start to lay out the pattern.

The pieces that you will not be using for the style you are making should be carefully folded up, paper clipped together and placed back in the pattern envelope so that they will not become confused with the pieces that you are using.

Let's take a look at your pattern pieces. You will find that each piece is plainly marked as to whether it is the dress back, dress front, sleeve, skirt front, skirt back, bodice back, bodice front or the facing.

Since the first garment we will be making is a shift or sheath dress, you will need only a front, a back, a neck facing, and an armhole facing. A facing is simply a piece of material which is cut in the same shape as the neck or armhole so that when stitched right sides together and then turned, it gives a finished edge.

You will notice that each piece has a long line near the center with an arrow or large dot at each end. It is usually labeled "lengthwise of goods." This is to make sure that you have your pattern placed correctly on the fabric before cutting. There will be more about this in the chapter on how to cut out your garment.

Your pattern may say "measure from the selvage." The selvage is the tightly woven edge of the material. Since your material is folded in half, you have two selvage edges when you are cutting out your pattern, one of which is hidden.

Some patterns will have double lines across them indicating where to lengthen or shorten that segment.

Now you will notice that a border has been drawn around each piece of pattern—in the form of a dotted line. This is usually ⅝" from the edge and is called the "stitching line." This line makes it very simple to know exactly where to stitch. You will use your tracing wheel to mark this so you will have no trouble stitching on the exact line.

You will notice, too, that there are little notches marked along the outer edge of the pattern—sometimes one notch, sometimes two or more. These all have a definite meaning, as you will see, and wherever there is a single notch it will match another piece of pattern with a single notch. Where there are two notches, there will be another set of double notches to match it. These notches are your guide in knowing exactly where to join your pieces of cloth.

Finally you will find at various intervals, three lines—two broken lines and a solid line—converging in a point, with the center solid line marked, "fold here". These are "dart lines" indicating that a dart must be taken here to give shape to the garment. In a fitted dress they are usually at the bustline, at the waist front, at the waist back and shoulder.

There are easy ways to mark all the things you will need on your material, but for now this is enough to show you that a pattern is really not so formidable but only a very simple blueprint for making a dress as professional looking as if you had gone to a very expensive couturière.

Now lay your pattern aside while we talk about all the other things you will need to know before you start making your first dress— how to pick your fabric, how to adjust the pattern to your individual measurements, how to lay out and mark your pattern, how to cut it, and finally, basic stitches and types of seams you will need.

CHAPTER 3

ALL ABOUT FABRICS
HOW TO CHOOSE YOUR OWN

Which Fabrics Are Right For You? Which Colors? — Including Fabric Chart

There are fabrics which are good for you and fabrics which you should avoid because they emphasize figure faults. They have either the wrong texture, pattern, or color. And color can affect emotion, either cheering you or depressing you.

It is just as important for you to learn to judge the right and wrong materials for your personal wardrobe as it is to know the right lines of the patterns you buy. The right fabric can enhance your beauty. The wrong one can ruin everything you have done to pick the right pattern with the right lines and styling.

Part of the joy of sewing is being able to pick fabrics that bring a lift to your feelings and give you a sense of assurance. You know your look best. Colors can make you look glowingly healthy and vibrant. The wrong color can make you look sallow or florid.

Walk down the aisles of the yard goods section of your favorite department store. Look at the hundreds of bolts of cloth, the many, many types of weaves, textures, the myriad of colors, the number of synthetics. This should reassure you that you will be able to find the material with weave, color, and texture that seems just made for you, the exact material to do the things you want it to do. A chart in this chapter will be handy to refer to for checking the various properties of fabrics, their strong points and how to care for each, and the widths they come in.

BASIC TYPES OF FABRIC

As you look at the bolts of goods all around you, you will discover that basically there are only three categories:

Firm Woven Fabrics: These are the strong materials which hold their shapes and do not stretch easily: brocade, broadcloth, gabardine, corduroy, tweeds and twills, taffeta, and velveteen.

Soft Woven Fabrics: These are the soft finish materials which drape easily, but are also a little harder to work with, for they also stretch easily. They include silk crepe, jerseys, knits, and many of the newer synthetic fabrics. Save these for your second or third garment.

Sheer Woven Fabrics: These are the see-through fabrics which are difficult for beginners because they may be stretchy or delicate and hard to handle. They also may have to be completely lined to hide the construction. The transparent fabrics are chiffon, lace, georgette, voile and organdy.

There is also another way you can classify fabric, and that is by surface appearance. All cloth is either solid color or patterned, and patterns break down into large, medium or small design which may also be geometric, floral, or novelty. The geometric designs are usually sharp and crisp in outline—stripes, checks and plaids. The floral designs are sometimes very hazy and almost an abstract pattern. The novelty designs can be as varied as the imagination.

But the important thing is, what can you wear?

WHICH FABRICS ARE RIGHT FOR YOU?

If you are average you can wear almost anything you choose, but not everyone is so lucky.

If you want to look taller, slimmer: Stay away from shiny materials that reflect light, such as satins and chintzes. Stick with dull surface materials such as twills, broadcloths or gabardines. Stick with dull textures and hard finishes. Dull textures make the same area look smaller. Shininess increases the illusion of size. Avoid clinging jersey that hugs the figure.

For taller look

If you want to look shorter and heavier: Stay away from jersey and other fabrics that cling too much and point up any bony protrusions. Choose medium to heavy materials. Bulky textures tend to flesh you out and pad or at least hide the too slim silhouette. Shiny and satiny materials will also make you look heavier. So will stiff materials such as crisp taffeta. Velvets and other pile materials are good for you.

WHICH COLORS AND PATTERNS ARE RIGHT FOR YOU?

You can do the same thing with color and pattern that you have done with texture to achieve the look you want. All colors are classified as warm colors, cool colors, or neutral colors.

Warm Colors: These are the earth colors: reds, yellows, and oranges. Off-shoots of these colors are also warm—pink, salmon, coral and gold. Rich brown is also a warm color.

Cool Colors: These are the sky and grass colors, blues of all kinds and greens except for those that have a lot of yellow, such as chartreuse.

Neutral Colors: These are the colors that have no brightness in themselves but serve as good background for colorful accessories: black, gray, beige, and white.

If you want to look taller or slimmer: Choose the cool colors or the neutral colors, and use the warm colors only for accessories or accent color. Warm colors seem to come toward you, and make the figure look larger. Cool colors recede. The brightness or dullness of any color can make a difference in how slim you look. Stay away from bright colors. Just remember brightness adds to the size. So does lightness. The lighter colors make you look larger, the darker colors, smaller. But there is a law of diminishing returns. If you are very heavy, you will look smaller in a neutral brown or grey than a stark black which tends to stand out in too marked contrast to the backgrounds against which you will move. In general, solid colors make you look slimmer than patterns, but you can use patterns if you are very careful.

Pattern: For which pattern to choose to look taller or slimmer, use medium or small patterns in which there is a vertical motion, that is, the vertical lines seem to be stronger or dominate over the horizontal lines. Stripes, even when vertical, do not always give a slim look. Hold the material up to you for judging. Stay away from plaids except for tiny ones. If you choose flowers or novelty prints, the effect should be of a small overall design rather than a large attention getting pattern.

If you want to look shorter or heavier: Choose warm colors for your overall effect. They make your figure look larger, more filled out. Also very light colors will tend to make you look larger. A very good trick to cut your size is to use two colors for a two piece dress because color contrast makes you shorter and heavier. You can also achieve this with contrasting yokes in one piece dresses.

Pattern: To cut your size or make you look heavier, wear plaids, large stripes, large flowers or prints. You can have fun picking prints of every description; they're made for you.

For shorter, heavier look

If you are an average person: Color adventure awaits you if you are the average person, neither too tall, too short, too heavy, too thin, too pale, or too florid in skin tone. You can really let yourself go on color building moods like an actress.

Do you want to suggest gaiety and excitement? Use a lot of reds and pinks and oranges. People are drawn to those that wear warm colors and will be more apt to start a conversation with them at a party. These colors suggest an outgoing person who has confidence in herself.

Yellow signifies cheerfulness. It is another good color to draw people toward you.

Blue can also be an exciting color and has the added advantage that most men, if asked their favorite color, say blue, as any clerk can tell you. They pick it when shopping for women's gifts. Blue can highlight blue and green eyes and is flattering to most complexions. Try the variations of blue turquoise and aqua, to see what they do for you.

If you want to suggest a feeling of relaxation, try the moderate greens that represent the peace of all outdoors. You can also go in for dramatic combinations such as black and white which have a dynamic effect. Or pink and orange which are startling together, but combine beautifully. Try green and blue together in vibrant shades, and bright yellow against navy. Try pink against red.

Some women take the easy way out. Because they are afraid to experiment, they wear dark or neutral shades season after season. A constant fare of either bright or drab colors is about as interesting as pulling weeds! For looks that are alive and vital and as a means of bringing new excitement into your life, vary your choice of colors. Don't be afraid to try new color combinations. You may discover a new you and find that you have also conquered shyness.

There is only one way that you can really be sure a color is right for you. Hold it up to your face, and see in a mirror how it affects your skin tones. That, more than hair color, is the decisive factor.

For instance, a person with a great deal of yellow in her skin tone would look sallow in beige and light yellows and needs stronger, more vibrant colors.

The ruddy faced person must stay away from rosy colors that emphasize the redness of her complexion. Here is where the cool or more neutral colors would come into use.

WHAT TO WATCH FOR WHEN YOU ARE BUYING YOUR MATERIAL

There are certain practical things you need to know, questions you will want answered when you are selecting the fabric you are going to sew.

Unless you know what to look for, you might buy fabric that has to be straightened before it can be cut or require more care than you are willing to spend on it. The maintenance of a garment can often be far more costly than you planned. Also, certain fabrics require special handling when sewing.

Here are the things you will want to know:

Is the grain perfect? Fabric is made of threads woven together. There is a lengthwise grain and a crosswise grain. These should run at right angles to each other. A mistake you can make in buying cloth is to choose cloth that is imperfect in grain, that is, the crosswise threads are not perfectly perpendicular to the lengthwise ones. You can usually see with the naked eye whether the crosswise threads run uphill instead of going in a straight line at a right angle to the selvage edge of the material.

It is important to pick material with perfect grain because your dress will never hang straight if it is cut on a slight bias instead of with the grain perfect. It will twist on your body and pull to one side or the other.

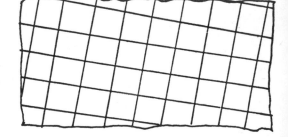

Fabric printed off grain

36

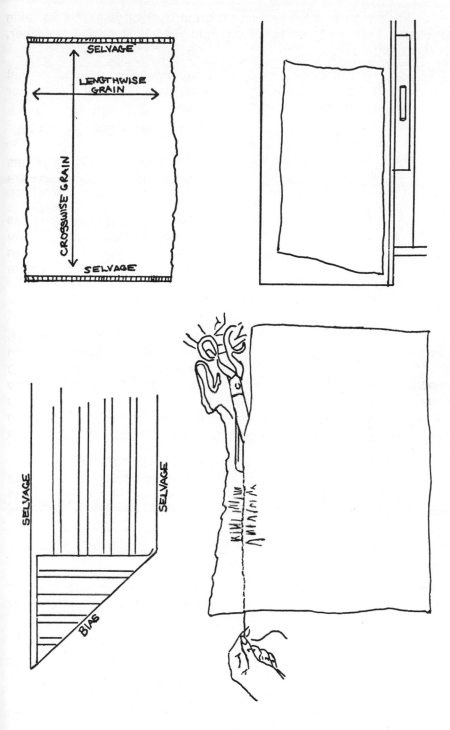

Checking for straightness of grain

To test whether a fabric has true grain you can do one of three things. But first you must straighten the end of the cloth, if needed. Pull a crosswise thread near the end of the material and cut along that line. Then you can place the material on a table end to see if the edge of the material is as straight as the edge of the table. Another way is to fold the end of the material diagonally—after you have straightened the end as above—so that the lengthwise thread falls across the crosswise thread forming a triangle. If it does not fall in place perfectly and the lengthwise grain refuses to coincide with the crosswise thread, you know you will have to straighten the material before cutting it. A third way is to fold the fabric lengthwise so the selvages match. Then if the folded cut end doesn't match and one corner juts above the other, it's off grain. Directions for straightening grain are in the chapter "How to Cut Your Pattern." There will be occasions when you cannot get material with perfect grain. But, to avoid extra work, you should try to find it whenever you can.

How crease resistant is it? By making a little crease in the fabric and pressing it down with your finger nail you can usually determine whether the material you are looking at will wrinkle easily. If a wrinkle appears immediately, it is a bad risk. Linens and some cottons, unless treated, are wrinkle prone. Synthetics are usually crease resistant. There are certain crease resistant finishes that manufacturers use. Look for these labels: (these are only some of the trade names)

Disciplined: A finish that not only gives crease resistance but also soil, mildew, and perspiration resistance.

Everglaze: This is a trademark that identifies materials that have been treated for crease, stretch, and crease resistance.

Perma-Pressed: A finish made by baking the material causing it to be crease-resistant and fast drying.

Wrinkle-Shed: A name given to a finish which resists mildew and sheds soil as well as shedding wrinkles.

Is it color fast? Even though you don't plan to wash the material you have to consider whether it will fade in cleaning or if exposed to the sun.

Many labels will say color fast meaning that it has gone through dyeing process to keep the color intact in laundering, dry cleaning, or exposure to sun. Other names you will see which tell you the same thing are Vat Dyed or Avisco Integrity.

Will it shrink? There are many shrinkage control finishes. But even with these finishes, there still can be a slight shrinkage. This is not enough to cause concern.

(If fabric is labelled "guaranteed preshrunk" or "ready to sew" it needs no further treatment. Other guarantees are:

Sanforized: Meaning the fabric has been treated not to shrink more than 1% when washed and used on cottons and cotton blends.

Sanforian: Similar process used on woolens.

Sanforset: Similar process used on rayons.

Zeset: Anti-shrinkage finish on rayon and cotton.

Lanaset: Shrinkage control used on wool.

Redmanized: Process used on synthetics, cotton, and wools.

Which is the right side of the fabric? Sometimes it's difficult to know which side of the fabric is the right side. Wool and silk are folded with their right side inside. Cotton is usually folded with its right side outside. But sometimes material is not folded but rolled on a bolt. Silk and wool are usually rolled with the right side underneath.

If you still are unsure, a good clue to follow is that the selvage edge is smoother and more perfect on the right side. Any imperfections or irregularities in the material are usually on the wrong side.

Does it require special treatment in sewing? Certain fabrics present certain problems in handling while sewing. These may influence your choice when shopping.

See-through fabrics: Sheer fabrics can be damaged when sewn on the sewing machine, so tissue paper must be placed under the material to protect it from the feed dog. This means that when you cut your pattern out you will need to cut the tissue paper backing at the same time, basting and sewing both together. Later this can easily be torn away.

Crepe: Also needs tissue paper backing because of its tendency to stretch. Also it has a tendency to slip and slide so would not be recommended for beginners.

Jersey: While stitching on the machine, jersey must be stretched slightly in order to keep the thread in the seams from breaking later. Also extra work is required in finishing the seams with bias tape or zig-zag stitching.

Double Knits: Use same treatment as for jersey.

Lace: Usually must be completely under-lined with net or organza to give it body. Requires a simple pattern with few seams.

Velvet: Very difficult to handle because it's easy to leave marks in the fabric. It must not be stitched on the outside of the fabric, and it requires a needle board for pressing. Also you must be sure that the nap of all the pieces of your pattern run the same way.

Now let us take a look at a chart which can be a handy guide in helping you pick the fabric for your sewing project according to its width, its care, and its qualities:

FABRIC CHART

WIDTH	TYPE OF FABRIC	GOOD POINTS	CARE REQUIRED
Wool 54" or 60" width	Gabardine, jersey broadcloth, crepe flannel, tweed, twill.	Warm, wrinkle resistant. Wears well.	Dry clean unless labeled otherwise. Must be pressed with press cloth on right side.
Cotton 35" or 36"	Broadcloth, gingham, corduroy, velveteen, chambray, lace, denim, calico, pique.	Washable, long wearing, easy to iron. Strong and versatile. Withstands bleaching.	Use hot iron and press while damp.
Silk 39"	Brocade, taffeta velvet, moire, jersey, crepe, satin, chiffon, surah.	Luxurious, drapes well, used for formal wear, as well as luncheon or cocktail clothes.	Press with moderate iron and press cloth on right side. Dry clean, unless labeled otherwise.
Linen 35" or 36"	Dress linen, handkerchief linen, suiting, crash, cambric, damask.	Crisp looking, cool, absorbent.	Washable. Press on wrong side while damp. Use hot iron.
Rayon 36" 39" or 45"	Crepe, shantung, velvet, flannel, linen weave, satin.	Drapes easily.	Press with warm iron. Check label for care of garment.
Orlon 39" or 45"	Suiting, shantung, jersey, satin, crepe.	Soft to the touch, resists wrinkles, and damage from sun or moths.	Washable, in warm water. Must use warm iron, heat destroys fabric.
Dacron 39" 45"	Taffeta, plisse, batiste, tricot, suiting.	Won't stretch or shrink. Moth, mildew and sunproof. Crease resistant. Quick drying.	Iron gently with warm iron. Washable.
Acrilan 39" 45"	Suiting, flannel, jersey.	Does not stretch, sag or wrinkle. Warm and light weight.	Check label. Sometimes washable in warm water. Needs little ironing. Heat destroys fabric.
Acetate 39" 45" and 50"	Taffeta, bengaline, satin, surah, faille, jersey.	Soft, and easy to drape. Moth and mildew resistant.	Dry clean or hand wash. Roll in towel to dry. Press while damp with cool iron.

CHAPTER 4
FIGURE PROBLEMS
HOW TO ADJUST YOUR PATTERN TO THEM
Includes Your Individual Measurement Chart

No two people are exactly alike in their measurements. Pattern manufacturers do the best they can by making patterns according to figure types and variations within the figure types.

Even so, you are most unusual if you will not have to change the paper pattern in some way to conform to your individual requirement. Maybe the sleeve is too short or too long, or the shoulder is too wide. You may be too narrow across the back or too wide in the hips to use the pattern as is.

Therefore, before you start cutting, first you will need to fill out the **Individual Measurement Chart** in this chapter so that you can check each pattern piece before you pin it to the fabric. But remember when you are comparing your measurements with the pattern that the pattern has allowed extra material for seams. This is called "seam allowance." Check your personal measurements against the pattern measuring right up to the stitching line of the seam.

(When measuring the pieces of the pattern never go beyond the line for the seam allowance which is marked on all patterns.)

There is a second factor you must allow for. Since you will not be wearing your clothes skin tight, you must leave room for movement. This is called "allowance for ease." This has already been structured into your pattern.

If there is only a slight variation between the pattern measurements and your own measurement plus the allowance for ease, you can wait to make this minor adjustment after you have basted it.

Here are the allowances most pattern manufacturers give:

Bust: 4 inches extra for ease (2 inches across the front and 2 inches across the back) which would mean adding an inch to each piece of your pattern.

Hips: About 2 inches ease is allowed for the hipline (1 inch in front and 1 inch in back).

Bodice Length: At least ½ inch is allowed.

Sleeve Width: About 3 inches ease is allowed the width of the sleeve measuring at bottom of the armhole.

Elbow: 1 inch is minimum allowance to give ease of movement at elbow.

You will find other ease allowances in your individual measurement chart. You will notice there is no allowance for the waistline, but you may want to add ¼ to ½ inch allowance for comfort.

Individual measurements

When taking measurements, always wear the foundation garment that you will be wearing under the finished garment.

To measure your body to fill in the Individual Measurement Chart, first put on a perfectly plain fitted dress in which the seams under the arm fall in a straight line and the length is perfect all the way around. Then, in contrasting tailor's chalk, draw a straight line down the center front and center back, or stretch tape or cord or elastic along the center line, securing it carefully with pins or stitches.

(If you use tailor's chalk, don't panic, it will disappear at the touch of a steam iron.)

To check your side seam, put a weight on a string and see if the seam follows a straight line when you let the string hang from armpit to ankle bone. You may have to draw a new, straighter line with tailor's chalk or stretched tape.

Finally, a word about your hemline. If you do not have a hemline you are sure is straight and perfect, first measure from your waistline to the floor. Then make a mark on your dress or leg where you want the hemline to be. Now measure from the floor to that point, and subtract that amount from your floor to waist measurements, which must be taken at four points from waist to floor—center front, center back, right skirt seam, and left skirt seam.

Now you're ready to start measuring. Remember the paper pattern is the width of only half the front or back of you.

INDIVIDUAL MEASUREMENT CHART

BASIC MEASUREMENTS	YOUR MEASUREMENTS	ALLOWANCE FOR EASE	THE PATTERN MEASUREMENT
CHEST—Place tape around body, under arms and above your bust.	_____	1 inch	_____
BUST—Place tape around body and over fullest part of bust		4 inches	
Front (center line to side seam)	_____	1 inch	_____
Back (center line to side seam)	_____	1 inch	
WAIST—Place tape around smallest part of waist			
Front (center line to side seam)	_____		_____
Back (center line to side seam)	_____		_____
HIP—Place tape around body 7" below waistline.		2 inches	
Front (center line to side seam)	_____	½ inch	_____
Back (center line to side seam)	_____	½ inch	
SHOULDER WIDTH—Measure from neckline to tip of shoulder bone.			
Right shoulder	_____		_____
Left shoulder	_____		_____

SLEEVE

	YOUR MEASUREMENTS	ALLOWANCE FOR EASE	THE PATTERN MEASUREMENT
SLEEVE LENGTH			
a. Measure from shoulder bone to elbow	_____		_____
b. From elbow to wrist	_____		_____
c. From underarm seam to wrist	_____		_____
SLEEVE WIDTH		3 to 4 inches	
a. Upper arm—measure at armpit level around arm	_____		_____
b. Lower arm—around arm below elbow	_____		_____
c. Wrist measurement	_____		_____

VERTICAL BODICE MEASUREMENTS	YOUR MEASUREMENTS	ALLOWANCE FOR EASE	THE PATTERN MEASUREMENT

UNDERARM SEAM—Measure underarm to waistline, starting 1 inch from armpit.
  Right bodice seam
  Left bodice seam

SHOULDER TO WAISTLINE—Measure from shoulder seam down over fullest part of bust to waistline

½ inch to 1 inch

CENTER FRONT — Measure from hollow of throat to center of waistline

SHOULDER TO BUSTLINE—Measure from shoulder seam to highest point bust

BACK BODICE LENGTH—

½ inch to 1 inch

a. From center back neckline to center waistline
b. From right shoulder seam to waistline
c. From left shoulder seam to waistline

BACK BODICE

BACK BODICE SHOULDER WIDTH—Measure from center line to shoulder tip

UPPER BACK WIDTH — Measure across back 4 inches below neckline, from center line to armhole

SKIRT LENGTH—Measure from waistline to desired length
  Center front
  Center back
  Right skirt seam
  Left skirt seam

2½ to 3 inches for hem allowance

Now you are ready to make the pattern fit you perfectly, just as if you'd gone to a couturiere. All you have to do is compare your measurements to the measurements of the pattern, up to the stitch line, remembering, of course to leave room for ease, as we discussed.

Another thing you can do to test fit, is try the pattern on. Don't laugh. Some experts recommend, and I heartily approve, that your first dress fitting is actually to pin the pattern together, just as if you were sewing it, with pins and putting it on. Only then, will you have full understanding of the problems involved and also be able to see if the style needs any slight change to be more flattering.

Test fitting

You may see, for example, when the pattern has been tacked to you, that the neckline should be higher or lower.

Now to make specific alterations in the pattern, the important thing is to realize that there is nothing sacred about a pattern. Be prepared to slash cut it at strategic places and insert more tissue paper to reshape the pattern to your own needs. It's better to spoil tissue paper than expensive cloth. And you can always try on the paper pattern again to make sure you have the right fit for you. So be brave.

To Lengthen Bodice or Waist: Cut pattern straight across two or three inches above the waistline. Spread apart the required amount and put sheet of tissue paper underneath, pinning the pattern to the tissue paper. Trim tissue paper to conform to the lines of the pattern.

To lengthen bodice or waist

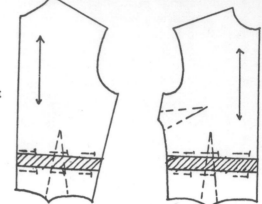

To Shorten Bodice or Waist: Make a fold across the pattern two or three inches above the waistline and pin down on pattern. If there is a dart at the waistline, redraw the dart to straighten the lines.

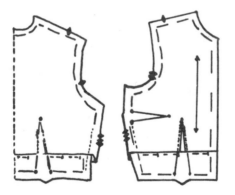

To shorten bodice or waist

To Shorten Back Bodice Only: First shorten the back bodice as explained above. Then fold, and make a tuck at the side seam of the front bodice taking in exactly the same amount you have taken in the back. Taper the tuck to nothing at the front of the bodice. Now put tissue paper lengthwise at the bodice front, and redraw pattern line to recapture true grain.

48

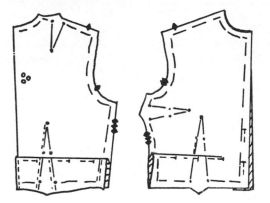

To shorten back bodice or waist

To Make Shoulders Narrower: Make a little tuck at the shoulder line halfway between neck and armhole, to take out the amount of pattern needed to fit your shoulder. Fold the tuck diagonally to a place just above the armhole notches. Pin pattern down and snip one or two places along the armhole seam allowance to make the pattern lie flat. Finally put small piece of tissue paper along shoulder line to redraw shoulder line.

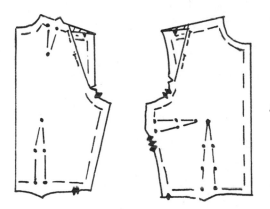

Adjustment for narrow shoulders

To Shorten or Lengthen Sleeve: First you decide if you need to add or subtract material above or below the elbow. Then either slash or fold pattern 3 inches above or 3 inches below the elbow, or both places, if necessary. Since your sleeve pattern will seem lopsided with darts at the elbow, measure bottom slash from the cuff edge, and upper slash from upper notches, which are evenly spaced.

49

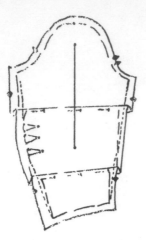

To shorten sleeve

To Make Shoulders Wider: Slash a diagonal line starting at shoulder line, one fourth way in from the armhole and tapering the dart or tuck to the armhole seam allowance, just above the notches. Spread apart, and add the required amount of tissue paper, and recut shoulder line. To make pattern lie smooth, pin a small tuck in the pattern armhole.

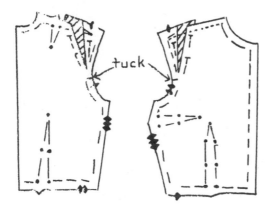

Adjustment for wide shoulders

To Make Adjustment For a Round Back — Also Called The "Dowager's Hump"

Slash pattern straight across the full part of the back, stopping a little above the armhole notch. Do not cut into the seam allowance. Spread pattern apart and insert tissue paper from the slash to the neckline, to straighten center back line. You have now enlarged the neckline and to restore it to the original size, take a tuck in the neckline exactly equal to the amount added at the center back. To make pattern lie flat, make tuck in armhole seam allowance.

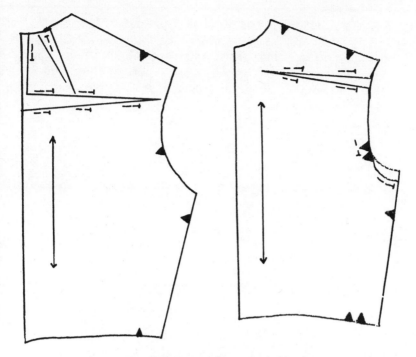

Adjustment for rounded back

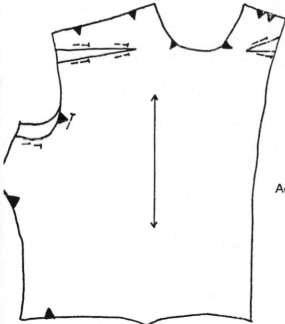

Adjustment for square shoulders

To Make Adjustment For Square Shoulders: Make slash front and back of bodice starting at armhole, or 1½ inch below the shoulderline cutting toward the center front and center back. Raise shoulder line the needed amount, pinning in tissue paper. Then add tissue paper to the lower armpit, lifting the underarm line the same amount the shoulder line was raised.

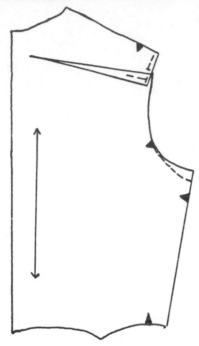

Adjustment for sloping shoulders

To Make Adjustment For Sloping Shoulders: Make a tuck in the armhole, of front and back starting one to two inches below the shoulder line and taper to nothing at center back. To bring the armhole back to normal, redraw bottom of the armhole, removing the same amount at the underarm as was removed by the tuck.

To Make Bustline Larger: First slash bodice front pattern vertically over the largest part of the bust from waistline to shoulder line, tapering to nothing at the shoulder seam. Then slash pattern horizontally just under the bust dart lines, tapering to nothing at the side seam allowance. Spread both cuts apart and place tissue underneath to fill in the needed amount. To restore the waistline to proper size, draw in a waistline dart in the slashed place, to be marked and then sewn into the material, when cutting your fabric.

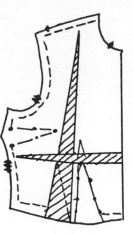

Adjustment for large bust

Adjustment For Short Neck: Make a horizontal fold in back of bodice, about 1 or 1½ inch below neckline and tapering to nothing at upper armhole. To make pattern lie flat, snip seam allowance at end of tuck.

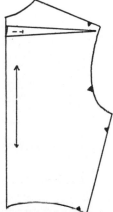

Adjustment for short neck

To Allow For Large Arms And Fullness Under Arms: Slash pattern on a slight bias from below armhole notch toward waistline. Spread apart to give the right amount of ease, and pin tissue paper to fill in. Then recut curve of the armhole.

If the dress has a sleeve, you must insert the same amount at both sides from underarm seam up to the notches. Your sleeve, where it is cut, will look like a toadstool. Slash each side from the underarm seam at the armpit to a distance two inches inward toward the center. Then cut in a right angle down toward the wrist or lower edge of the sleeve tapering to nothing. Spread sleeve the same amount as you did the armhole. Fill in with tissue paper, and recut armhole line of sleeve.

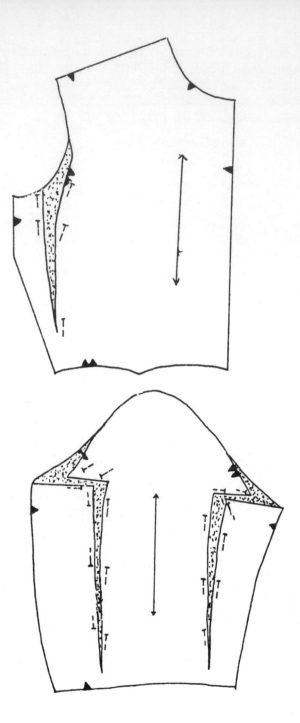

For large arm fullness

To Make Top Of Sleeve Wider: Slash verticle line from top of sleeve pattern toward elbow and spread apart to insert proper amount of tissue paper. Pin together to hold tight. Then, to adjust armhole to new sleeve size, pin piece of tissue paper to top of bodice side seams, front and back, adding half the extra width to the front and half to the back.

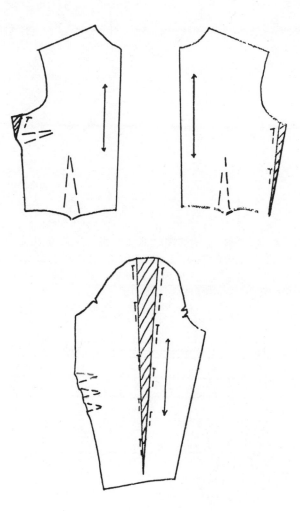

To make sleeves wider

To Add Width At Elbow—And Give More Room For Bending:
Slash sleeve vertically, beginning a fraction of an inch from the top, and slash down to within one inch from the bottom. Cut close to grainline marker for your guide line, then slash a horizontal line from the elbow to the vertical slash. Spread both cuts apart the required amount for comfort, and pin tissue paper under it, to hold it together for cutting pattern. Recut the elbow line, to conform to the original.

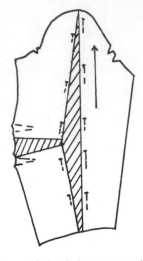

To add width at elbow

To Make Sleeve Narrower: Make a verticle fold on each side of cap of sleeve from top to bottom and redraw top of the sleeve, using the pattern as your guide. (Before making your folds you will want to transfer the curve to a piece of newspaper.)

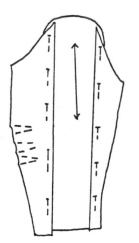

To make sleeve narrower

To Lower Pattern Bustline: Cut your pattern horizontally above the bustline dart, and insert a strip of tissue paper to put the bustline where it belongs. Then take up the slash by making a fold midway between the bustline and waistline to take up the equivalent of the tissue you have added.

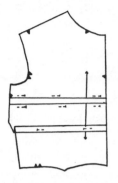

To lower bustline

For Hollow Chest: Make horizontal tuck straight across bodice four inches below neckline, taking out the necessary amount and tapering to nothing at armhole. Next, restore original grain line by redrawing center front line. By redrawing your center front line, you have made the neckline smaller. Therefore you must now add the same amount you removed from the neck front to the top of the neckline shoulder seam. Finally, you must redraw your shoulder and armhole line, using your pattern to guide you.

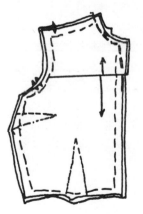

For hollow chest

To Make Neckline Larger: Don't hesitate to cut neckline deeper if you have a full face or full neck. But be sure to do the same thing to the facing.

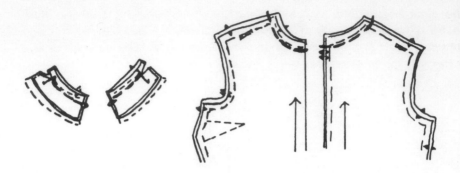

To make neckline larger

To Make Neckline Smaller: Pin tissue paper under the neckline, and draw a new neckline to hide a thin neck or make a more attractive line for a long neck. Don't forget, if you have lengthened the shoulder line at the neck, to do the same to the back of the bodice. Also, your front and back facings will have to be recut to match.

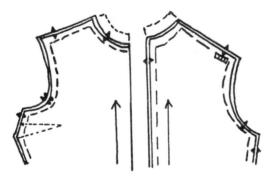

To make neckline smaller

To Lengthen or Shorten Skirt: Cut horizontal line straight across the skirt at the hipline 7 inches below waistline. Insert tissue paper to add required length. To shorten skirt make fold at the hipline, 7 inches below waistline and take up the required amount.

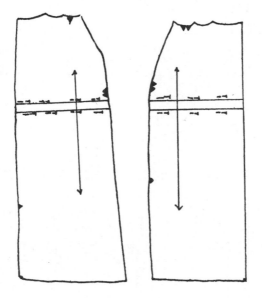

To lengthen or shorten skirt

To Increase Skirt or Dress Waistline: Slash skirt vertically from the waistline downward, starting at a point one-fourth of the way in from the side seams and tapering to nothing at the mid-skirt. Now slash the bodice upward tapering to nothing at a point parallel to the armpit. Insert tissue spread apart, and pin the allowance for ease. If most of your weight is in the front, and not in back, divide the increase by 2 and only use the front pattern. But if the weight is evenly distributed front and back, divide the amount needed by four and spread apart that much in front and the same amount in back.

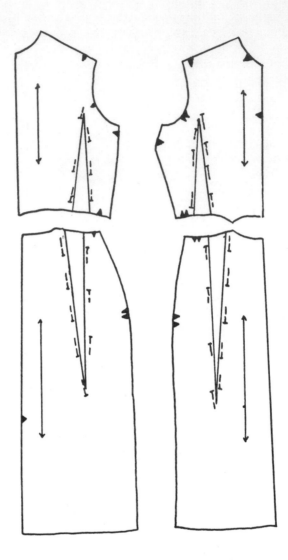

For larger waistline

To Increase Hipline: If your waistline does not need to be changed, but only your hipline, slash front and back skirt pattern vertically from hemline, cutting up to a point just below and to the inside of the waistline notches. Spread apart the proper amount. Make the side seam return to its normal line by taking a small tuck in pattern at the fullest part of the hip—7 inches down from the waistline—and tapering to nothing at the seam line.

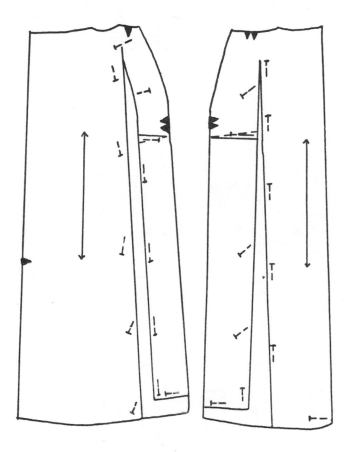

To increase hipline

To Adjust For Small Hips: Redraw the hipline front and back, and continue tapering the line along the side seam to the hemline. Divide the amount by four to see how much to take off on each of the two pieces of pattern.

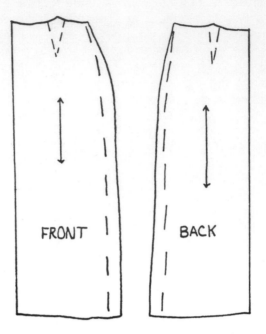

To adjust for small hips

CHAPTER 5
HOW TO CUT YOUR PATTERN

Directions for Straightening Fabrics. How to Lay Out and Mark Pattern for Sewing. Tips on Cutting.

You will get a feeling of power as you wield your scissors and cut out your first garment. But before you actually cut, there are a few things you must make sure of.

Is your material straight on the grain? The place to check the grain is at either end of your length of material. See directions for pulling a thread and testing for straightness of grain in Chapter 3. (For materials in which you cannot pull a thread, because of their texture, you may need another technique: For hard woven fabrics, snip through the selvage and tear the fabric carefully to the other selvage. If it is a jersey or other soft fabric, you should use a tailor's square or other object that has a perfect right angle such as a tablet or a newspaper, to draw your line for straightening the material. Just place one side of the object against the selvage edge, and you can mark a perpendicular line across the width of the material, using the adjacent side as your guide.)

If your material is off grain, which sometimes happens in the process of manufacturing—that is, the crosswise threads run at a slant instead of perpendicular to the selvage edge—you can sometimes straighten the grain without much trouble. Simply pull and stretch the cloth on the bias or diagonal in the opposite direction from which it is warped until it is straight.

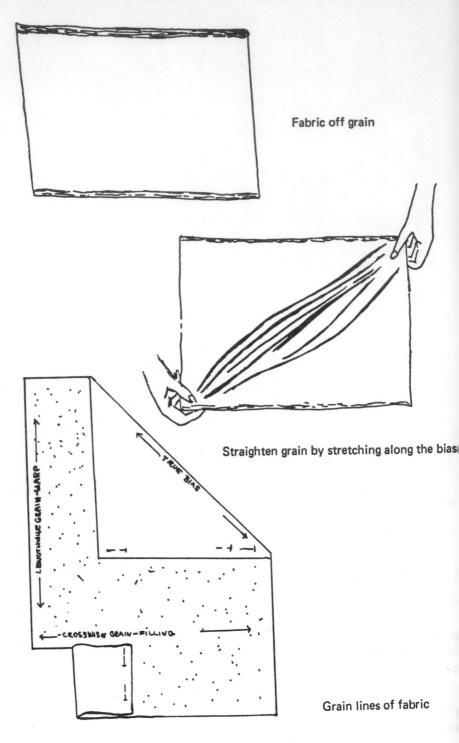

Fabric off grain

Straighten grain by stretching along the bias

Grain lines of fabric

LENGTHWISE GRAIN—WARP

TRUE BIAS

—CROSSWISE GRAIN—FILLING

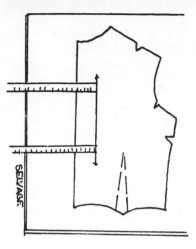

Measuring the grain line

Or you can steam press the fabric while gently pulling it and pinning it in place.

If the grain is too far off to be corrected by pulling on the bias, and the material is washable, you can fold the material lengthwise and baste the ends and selvages together the way they should be and then soak the material until wet through. Press while the material is still a little damp, and pull to straighten any additional amount necessary.

For woolens it is best to take it to a dry cleaner and have it steam pressed and straightened.

But if you must straighten the wool material yourself, here are the steps you must follow:

a. Snip through the selvage every three or four inches. Fold material lengthwise, wrong side out.
b. Baste along the selvage side and ends.
c. Roll material with a dampened sheet and leave for 8 hours.
d. Press with steam iron while still basted.

Does the material need shrinking? If you are using linen or cotton which has not been preshrunk but which you intend to have laundered, soak the material in hot water for one hour; then dry and press.

Is your pattern or material wrinkled? If so, press the pattern pieces gently with a luke warm iron, and then press the folds out of the material.

Laying Out Your Pattern: (Use cutting board or table.)

You are now ready to lay the pieces of the pattern on the folded length of your material, which should always be folded to have the wrong side up. You have put aside the pieces of the pattern that you will not need. You have also marked the cutting layout for the style of the garment you are going to make. (See Chapter 2.)

This layout has been worked out by the pattern company so there will be no waste of material. Lay the pattern on the length of material as indicated making sure that you keep the grain perfect by measuring with tape or ruler from the selvage edge to the line on your pattern indicating the lengthwise grain of the fabric. You must measure from both ends of this line because both ends must be the same distance from the selvage edge.

Some pieces will be marked "place on fold." This means the single marked line must be pinned on the fold of the fabric. All cutting lines of a pattern are indicated by a double line or a heavy black line. You should cut right on this line or between the double lines.

When you do not have a layout guide, or you are changing the style so that your pattern no longer fits the layout, or you must make a new layout because you are using fabric in which the nap must all run the same way, here are the general rules to follow in laying out your pattern pieces:

1. Place the large pieces of the pattern on the material first, and fit the smaller pieces in the left over spaces.

2. Use the pieces marked "place on fold" first to be sure these pieces are on the folded edge of the material.

3. If you use fabric with nap or with printed pattern which has a top and bottom, you must lay all the pieces of the pattern going in the same direction. Short napped fabrics such as velveteen and corduroy are cut to have the nap going up toward the face. Long napped fabrics such as camels hair should be cut with the nap going down towards the hem. To determine which way the nap runs, rub your hand on the surface. If it feels rough the nap is up. If smooth, the nap is down.

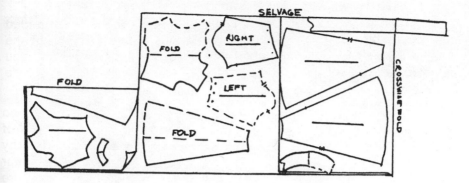

Pattern layout

If your material has a large pattern or plaid, you will need to buy ½ yard more than the pattern calls for to allow for matching the pattern. Stripes and checks must be matched at the seam line to give a professional appearance. Be sure all notches which are to meet each other fall on the same color stripe, or the same horizontal and vertical line of the plaid. Check distance from each end of "lengthwise of goods" line to selvage edge to make sure they are equi-distant. This makes sure your pattern is on the grain.

You are now ready to pin the pattern to the fabric.

Use dressmaker pins or silk pins. Silk pins, which are finer are necessary for velvet, taffeta, or any other fabrics that mar easily.

Insert the pins so that they will hold the pattern securely to the material, putting the pins in at the ends of the pattern first and then pinning along the grain or seam lines. When you have finished pinning, check to make sure all pieces are on and all the facings. Also check your pattern again to make sure you are cutting the right number of pieces for each part of the pattern.

Cutting Your Pattern:

At last you are ready to cut. Use your 7 or 8 inch cutting shears, but never use your pinking shears for cutting out your pattern. They will be used later for finishing seams of firmly woven goods.

Do not open your scissors too wide or close them all the way as you cut. Cut from the middle of the blade forward, and use a sliding motion so that you do not have to lift the fabric from the table.

Whenever you come to a notch which is shown indented on the edge of the pattern, cut it the opposite way making a notch outside the pattern line to protect your material. If there is excess margin around the pattern, don't be concerned because the excess tissue will fall away as you cut the pattern.

Cut notches outside pattern line

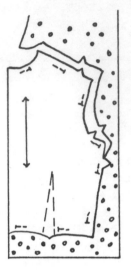

Marking Your Pattern:

Now you are ready to use your tracing wheel and dressmaker's carbon paper—using contrasting color to your fabric—to transfer the sewing instructions on the pattern to your cut out pieces of fabric. This is a great boon to easy accurate sewing. You will hear about other methods of marking patterns, such as making tailor's tacks, and the pin-and-chalk method, but the most precise and easy to follow markings are made by the tracing wheel and carbon paper method, which I recommend.

Place the carbon on the table face up underneath the fabric. Then place another piece of carbon face down between the pattern and the top of the folded fabric. Now trace all darts, tucks, stitching lines, fold lines of darts, button holes, pocket markings, and other guide marks with your tracing wheel, following the lines marked on your pattern. In a few minutes you will have marked both sides of your pattern at the same time with marks which will be on the wrong side of the garment. Your pieces of cloth will be as plainly marked as the pattern itself and will be as easy to follow as a blueprint.

Use tracing wheel with carbon between pattern and wrong side of fabric to transfer sewing instructions

Your garment is now ready for basting. If you have used material that is very stretchy or loosely woven, you will need to run a line of machine stitching, called stay stitching around the outer edge of all your pieces of pattern. This should be about ⅛ inch outside the seam line which you have marked with your wheel. This will prevent the cut edge from stretching or raveling.

You will see how true it is that a stitch in time saves nine. You'll be surprised at how fast these pieces are going to spring into place and make a beautiful garment.

But to have that beautiful finish, you're going to need the right stitches.

CHAPTER 6
BASIC STITCHES AND HOW TO SEW A SEAM

The longest trip starts with a single step, and the sewing of every dress, from the longest to the shortest, starts with a single stitch.

As promised in the Introduction, even if you have never held a needle in your hand before, you should be able to go about the making of your first dress with confidence.

And you can do it as you read this book.

So, take out your thread and your needle, and let's begin to get acquainted with them. You should not sew with more than about 15 inches of thread at a time. Eventually you will be able to gauge 15 inches with your eye, but this time measure to see what 15 inches looks like.

You have seen even experienced sewers stab at the eye of the needle before getting it through the eye. That's because they have not cut off the fuzzy end from the tip of the thread. The way to get rid of the fuzz is to cut it off with your trimming scissors holding your scissors diagonally to make a sharper point, and an easier tip to thread.

Now hold the needle in your left hand if you are right handed, and turn it until you see the light through the eye. Then push the thread through the eye.

Usually you will make one end of the thread longer than the other because you nearly always sew with a single thread. Only where great strength is needed, such as sewing buttons, use a double thread. In either case, you make the knot in the thread the same way.

Tying a Knot: Hold the end of the single or double threads between the thumb and the middle finger. if you have trouble holding the thread, dampen the middle finger. Now wrap the end of the thread around the middle finger, and roll it off with your thumb. As you roll it off, catch it between your first finger and thumb and pull the long end of the thread with your other hand, automatically tightening the knot.

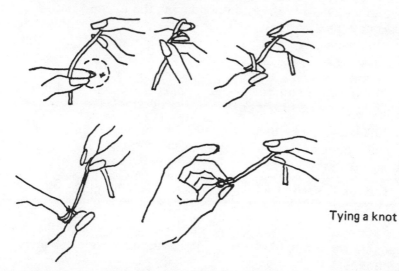

Tying a knot

There are all kinds of stitches. It is important to use the most efficient stitch for the particular need. Practice each of the stitches right now as we talk about them. You will need to know how to baste, how to sew and finish a seam. Also a few tips on the easy use of your sewing machine are in order.

On the matter of seams, you will need to know when to use a plain seam, when to pink a seam, when to overcast, and when to make a French seam; and the difference between a French seam and a flat felled seam, and between a French seam and a mock French seam. There are many other points we will take up in this chapter, but as we said, one stitch at a time.

BASIC STITCHES

Basting: Basting is temporary stitching used to hold pieces of fabric together while fitting and stitching. You are making your first dress. You have cut out your pattern pieces and are ready to join the shoulder seams together. First you would hold the two pieces together with a few pins; then you would sew the two pieces together with long stitches called basting stitches. These stiches should be ¼ to ½ inch long. They may not be perfect since they are going to be removed.

71

To make a basting stitch, push your needle in and out in a straight line close to but not on the stitching line because it is harder to remove basting if it has been stitched over.

Hold your needle between your first finger and your thumb of your right hand, if you're right handed, with the second finger resting on the needle next to the first finger. Now push the needle through the material using your middle finger which is protected by a thimble, bringing it back out about ¼ of an inch from where you inserted it—your eye will eventually learn to gauge distances. As soon as the needle is half way out of the material again catch it, and pull it through with your thumb and forefinger.

While your right hand is doing the sewing your left hand is holding the edges of the fabric together and in place. As you sew, you will gently guide the fabric.

There are several kinds of basting, depending on the job the stitches must do:

Even Basting: This is used when there will be strain on the seams such as while fitting the garment. Make the stitches ¼ inch long on both sides of the fabric.

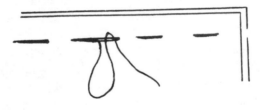

Simple basting

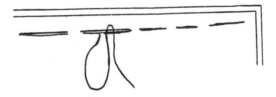

Uneven Basting: Faster and easier. If there is no strain on the seam take longer stitches on top and a short one to pull the thread through.

Diagonal Basting: Necessary for holding slippery material such as satin or for keeping several layers of fabric in place. Take short diagonal stitches on the top side so that the under side will have vertical stitches which are at right angles to the edge of the material.

Slip Basting: Useful in matching stripes, plaids, or other designs. Working on the right side of the fabric, turn under the seam allowance of one piece of the material, and press it down flat. Then pin this over the matching design on the other piece of the material. The important thing is to make stitches which will enable you to open up the material and stitch your seams on the sewing machine on the wrong side. Therefore take a small stitch in the very fold which you have made by pressing, and take a small stitch in the under piece of fabric continuing this line along the folded edge. If you keep the line straight, no stitches will show on the right side.

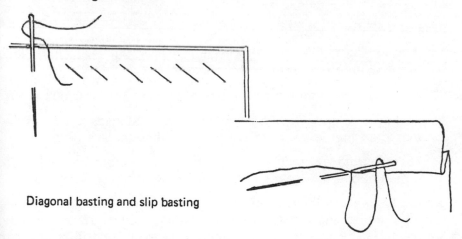

Diagonal basting and slip basting

Pin Basting: Quick and easy technique if you don't need to baste before machine stitching. For materials that are easy to work with such as firm woven cottons or bonded materials. Simply pin the material together, placing pins at right angle to the edge of the material in an even row. The important thing is to make sure that the pins are holding the material together exactly where you want the stitching to be.

Machine Basting: You can save time in basting any firm material if you pin baste as mentioned above and then set your sewing machine at the longest stitch. This is, however, harder to remove. You will need to cut the top thread at short intervals and pull out the bottom thread—at least every inch.

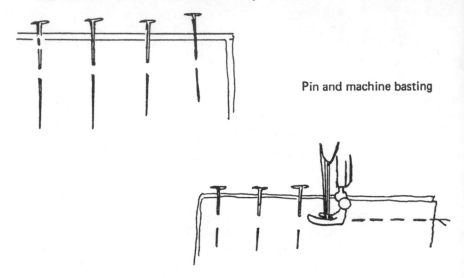

Pin and machine basting

General Tips For Basting:

1. Do not pull the thread tight while basting, but leave it slightly loose so that the fabric won't pucker.

2. Use contrasting thread so it's easier to see when you pull it out.

3. At the end of the line of basting use several stitches to secure the thread so that you won't have to waste time making a knot.

4. To keep from leaving marks in the fabric, do not pull out the whole thread at one time, but cut the basting stitches every few inches.

5. Always wear a thimble on the middle finger to push the needle through. Sewing without a thimble is slow going. Use either side or end of thimble to push against, whichever feels right for you.

74

Hand Stitches

Hand stitches are the permanent stitches which remain in your garment so you will make them as neat as possible. Again, the use determines the kind of stitch used.

Running Stitch: This is the most commonly used stitch. It is used when making anything by hand such as delicate baby clothes. It is also used for mending or quilting. Or in gathering material to make a ruffle. Simply take several short even stitches about ⅛th of an inch in and out of the fabric before pulling the thread through.

Back Stitch: Needed for making a hand stitch that is as firm as a sewing machine stitch. First take a stitch—⅛th of an inch long—

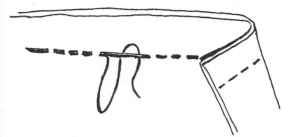

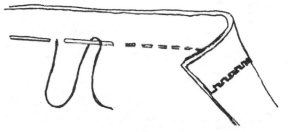

Running stitch and back stitch

in and out of the fabric and draw the thread through. Then going back half way, make another ⅛th inch stitch, putting the needle back through and bringing the thread out 1/16th of an inch in front of the first stitch. This way you will have overlapping stitches each ⅛th of an inch long with the strength of stitches half the size.

Stitches Used For Hemming

Hemming Stitch: Use small slanting stitches catching a few threads in the main fabric and passing the needle through the folded edge. Repeat over and over working from the main fabric through the fold of the hem.

Slip Stitch: Used every place you don't want stitches to show on the top side of the garment, such as for facing, but where strength isn't important. Starting with the folded fabric near the edge, make a firm stitch to anchor the knot. Then pick up only one or two threads of the main fabric underneath the fold passing the needle through the fold in a long or short stitch to suit your need. The main point is that no stitches show on top.

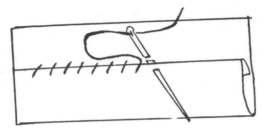

Hemming stitch and slip stitch

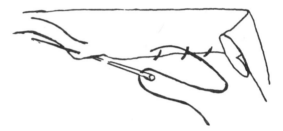

Catch Stitch: (or cross stitching). Used in hemming heavy fabrics where a raw edge can not be turned under. Working from left to right take a small stitch in the main fabric. Take the second stitch a little above the fold in the folded fabric; then take the third stitch back down in the main fabric. Cross stitches are a little farther apart than stitches in lighter weight fabrics. You may want to pink the edges before you start to further keep the material from raveling, and to leave less of a ridge.

Whipping Stitch: Used in making rolled hems such as on fine hand-kerchiefs or under garments. With the wrong side of the material up, facing you, roll the edge slightly with the thumb and first finger of your left hand. With the needle in a slanting position, make small diagonal stitches through the rolled edge of the material to hold the edge in place. Lace edging can also be attached to the rolled edge in the same operation, while you are whip stitching.

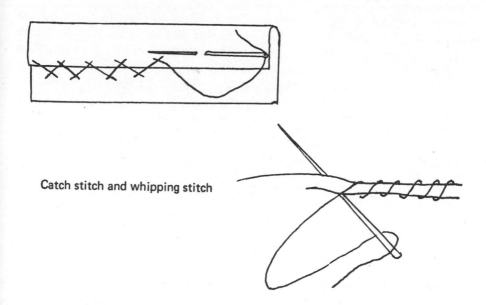

Catch stitch and whipping stitch

Overhanding: The most invisible stitch you can make, because of its shallowness. Can be used where strength as well as invisibility is important, too, such as in patching or attaching lace to a garment. Place the edges that are to be joined with the right sides together on the inside. You will have two ridges, or edges facing up. Now make tiny stiches over the two edges joining them together. Catch up only one or two threads on each edge.

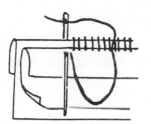

Overhand stitch

Getting To Know Your Sewing Machine

Don't be afraid of your sewing machine. Most beginners get panicky about running a sewing machine because they are afraid of ruining their material and their fingers.

The way to protect your fingers is: never put either hand in front of the needle but always to the side and well away from it. Always stop the machine before you make any adjustment of your material, or before checking to see if your needle is threaded properly.

As for the second point, ruining the material, the best way to learn to stitch is to practice running the machine using lined tablet paper instead of cloth. First try it with no thread in the machine. Just practice running the needle along the straight lines.

How to Practice on Paper without Thread: First, put your sheet of paper under the needle with the line running toward you. Now reach your right hand back of the post holding the needle and lower the lever which controls the presser foot. The presser foot is the name for the split prong metal piece which holds the material firm while you are sewing.

You always start by inserting the needle into the material first before lowering the presser foot. This assures you that the seam starts exactly where you want it to.

Start the machine by grasping the wheel with your right hand and slowly turning it toward you. Then as you press either the foot pedal or the knee pedal, depending on which type machine you have, the machine will start to stitch, pulling the sheet of paper through to the back. Keep your left hand resting on the paper to guide it in a straight line as it moves to the back of the machine.

The amount of pressure used on the control determines the speed with which the paper flows through. Don't be afraid to change the speed as you experiment and learn to follow the straight lines of the paper.

When you get to the end of the line stop by lifting your foot or knee from the control, touch the wheel as it slows and when it comes to a complete stop, lift the presser foot and withdraw the paper.

Practicing with Thread: Various machines require different techniques of threading. Your machine will have instructions for threading; if they have been lost, you can go to a store that sells your brand and ask for help.

Practice threading the machine and the bobbin until it becomes second nature to you. The bobbin rests in a case in the base of the machine, and the thread from it comes up and forms a loop over the thread from the needle which makes the stitch in the fabric.

When the machine is threaded you must remember always to draw thread to the back. The needle thread should go between the prongs of the presser foot and then is pulled to the back. Do this even before you insert the needle into the material. This is to keep the thread from becoming knotted when you begin to sew.

78

The bobbin thread that comes up through the feed dog should also be pulled to the back.

The length of your stitch is controlled by a stitch regulator on the side of your machine, and you will learn the stitch best for the material you are using. The main thing is not to use too tight a stitch because it would be hard to rip and might have a tendency to pucker.

Practice using the machine on a firm piece of material such as denim or gingham to begin with, and then experiment with other types of material changing your stitch as needed.

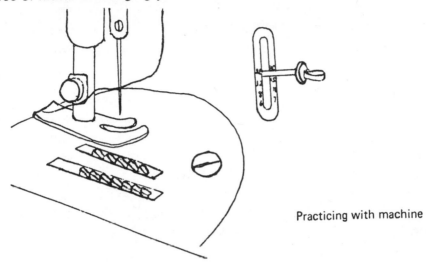

Practicing with machine

HOW TO SEW A SEAM

You can have professional looking clothes from the very beginning if you take pride in your seams. The mark of the amateur is that seams are not neat. They are pulled or puckered, and they draw attention to themselves instead of being an inconspicuous part of the garment.

To follow the rules of the expert, baste everything where there is a chance you will not be able to stitch straight without basting. Just as important, press each seam open as you go before you join it with another seam. Most patterns allow ⅝ths of an inch seam allowance, and it is wise to stick to this. Otherwise you'll have slight variations in the fit of your garment.

The kind of material determines the kind of seam you will need. For example, you may want to use a welt seam if you are using heavy fabric. You may want a double-stitched seam on a cotton garment that is going to be washed often. Tailored blouses and slacks require flat felled seams, and filmy materials require French seams. As you plan your garment, make a mental note of the kind of seams you are going to use.

Study your pattern. This will also help you decide which seams to use.

Also, fabrics that ravel easily or are bulky require special seam finishes, such as pinking, overcasting or binding. Even though you are not going to use them all on your first dress, you should study them all now so that you will be familiar with them and know where to find them when you need them.

Plain Seam: You will use this seam more than any other because it is the standard way to sew two pieces of fabric together. Pin or baste two pieces of material together, right sides on the inside, and machine stitch or hand stitch in a line ⅝ths of an inch from the edge. For ordinary material, plain seams should be pressed open.

Flat Felled Seam: This is used for men's shirt and women's sports clothes. First you sew the two seams together in a plain seam but with wrong sides together. Next press both seams to one side. Now trim the under seam allowance to ⅛th inch, and fold the top seam over it turning under the raw edge. Now top stitch close to the folded edge.

French Seam: Used for sheer fabrics such as organdy or chiffon and for dainty sewing such as baby clothes. First you make a plain seam with the wrong sides facing each other. This should be a very narrow seam with the stitches no more than ¼th to ⅜th inches from the edge of the fabric. Now trim both seam allowances to ⅛th inch and press. Then turn the material wrong side out and stitch to cover the raw edge—¼th inch from the folded edge.

Mock French Seam: First make a plain seam as for ordinary sewing with the right sides together, and leaving ⅝ths seam allowance. Now turn the raw edges under, toward each other so that there is no raw edge exposed. Top stitch close to this folded edge.

Eased Seam: Used frequently at elbow of a sleeve seam and other places where one seam is longer than the other and this fullness is needed to give ease. Take running stitches along the seam line of the longer piece of material and draw the thread until it is the same length as the shorter piece. Then pin the seams together with pins across the seam line so that you can sew over the pins, keeping the gathered side on top.

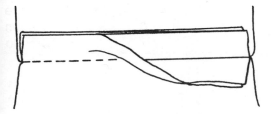

Plain seam

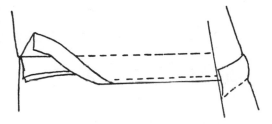

Flat felled seam

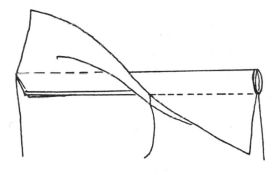

French seam

Eased seam

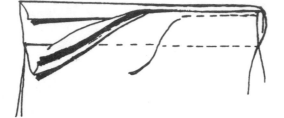

Mock French seam

Double Stitched Seam: This is simply a variation of the plain seam reinforced because of hard wear or because the fabric is sheer. Sew a second row of stitching in the seam allowance ⅛th inch from the first row of stitching.

Top-Stitched Seam: For re-inforcement of a plain seam where flatness is required. Can also be decorative. After stitching the plain seam, press seam allowances to one side, and stitch fabric on the right side close to the seam.

Double-Top Stitched Seam: Used on tailored garments for a decorative finish. After making a plain seam, press seam allowances open; and sewing on the right side of the fabric, stitch lines on each side of the seam line at the desired distance.

Slot Seam: Used as a decorative touch to show a line of contrasting color or contrasting grain of fabric. Instead of making a plain seam, simply turn under, and press the seam allowances on both edges. Place them side by side with the folded edges almost touching, and baste them to a strip of contrasting fabric which is the full length of the seam and a comfortable width to handle —about 1½ inches. Stitch on the right side of the material at the desired distance from the folded edge. In order to be sure your contrasting strip is on the grain, mark the center line with a basting stitch before inserting it.

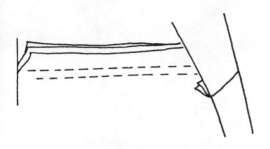

Double stitched seam

Top-stitched seam

Double-top stitched seam

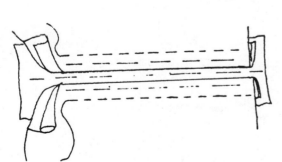

Slot seam

Lapped Seam: Used for yokes and other places where material is joined and stitched on the right side. First turn under the seam allowance on the piece of the garment that is to remain on top, and pin over the under piece so that both seam allowances match. Baste together before stitching the desired distance from the edge.

Welt Seam: This is a good seam for heavy fabrics where you don't want the thickness of a flat felled seam. Make a plain seam joining the two right sides of the fabric together. Then trim one seam allowance ⅛th inch from the stitching line. Finally press the wider seam allowance over the trimmed seam and stitch down, leaving the raw edge showing.

Corded Seam: Use as a decorative touch in clothing and in home furnishings such as bedspreads, draperies and slip covers. First insert the cord in a bias strip of material, and stitch close to the cord as possible. A zipper foot or cording foot is used for this. Then insert the encased cord between the two pieces of material which have right sides together—and all the seam allowances face the same way. Now, on the wrong side of the material stitch as close to the cord as possible.

Piped Seam: Same as corded seam without the cord. Take a folded piece of bias fabric or tape and insert between the seam allowances of two pieces of material whose right sides are placed together. Baste and stitch so that an even amount of the piping will remain showing.

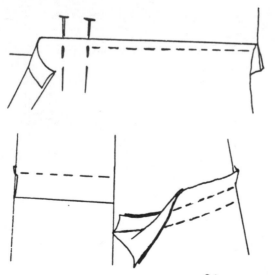

Lapped seam

Welt seam

84

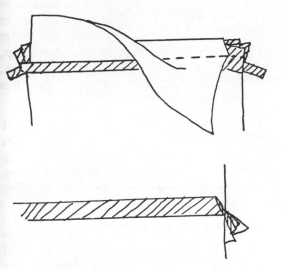

Corded seam

Piped seam

SEAM FINISHES

Pinked Edge: Cut along outer edge of seam (the raw edge) with your pinking shears to leave a saw tooth edge. Some pinking scissors produce a scalloped edge if you prefer. Pinking is the most popular form of seam finishing for fabrics that do not ravel easily. This will keep them from fraying, looks neat, and assures that there is less of a ridge line.

Stitched Edges: A good finish for light and medium weight fabrics that ravel. After you press the plain seam open, turn under the raw edge ¼th inch and stitch along the fold. Use machine or hand stitch.

Single Overcast Edges: An easy finish for raw edges and also useful in holding raw edges together. Simply hold the edges of the seam together, and take slanting stitches over the top edge putting the needle through both thicknesses at the same time. This may also be used to finish each edge of the seam separately if desired, in which case the seam is pressed open first.

Edges Overcast Together: Press the seams together and overcast as if they were one, making the stitches small slanting stitches over the edge about ¼th inch apart. Be sure to leave the thread loose to avoid puckering.

Machine Overcasting: For heavy or medium weight materials that ravel easily, you may prefer to use your machine for overcasting. Press seam apart, and stitch close to the edge using your zig zag stitch or overcaster.

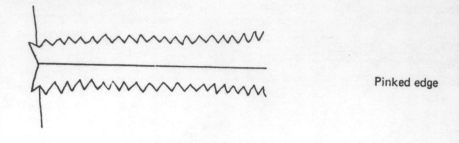

Pinked edge

Stitched edge

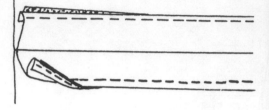

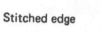

Single overcast edges

Edges overcast together

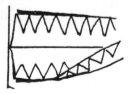

Machine overcasting

86

Bound Edge: Best for heavy fabrics that fray easily and also for un-lined coats or suits. Buy regular binding already folded or press into a fold. Then after pressing the seam open, slip the edge of the seam into the tape, and stitch close to the edge of the tape.

Rolled Edge: This is the best finish for sheer fabrics and dainty materials used in children's clothes. First trim the seam allowance to ⅜ths inch. Then using your thumb and forefinger, roll the two thicknesses of material toward the seam line making a tiny roll which you can fasten by sewing with overcast stitches, including the whole roll within the stitch.

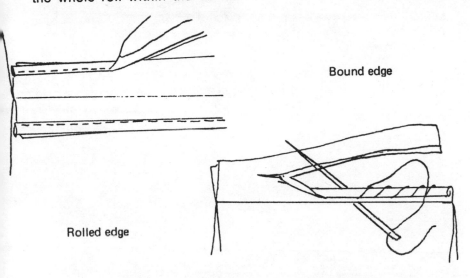

Bound edge

Rolled edge

GENERAL TIPS FOR SEWING A SEAM:

Seam allowance: Follow the recommendations made by your pattern on seam allowance. If no direction is given allow ⅝ths of an inch.

Basting: Basting always pays off in a better fit and time saved in trying on the garment before you stitch it. If you don't baste you may find yourself having to rip out many seams to make changes.

Press: Make a rigid rule of pressing every seam as soon as it is stitched and before it is joined to another seam. Keep your ironing board up as you sew.

Sheer fabrics: When sewing on sheer fabrics, lace, satin, or any other fabric that tends to slip or pucker, place a strip of tissue paper under the fabric, and tear off when you are through stitching.

Joining crossed seams: Be sure that both seams are pressed open before joining.

Jersey: When stitching on jersey, in order to keep the material from stretching, you will need to use preshrunk tape. Lay it on top of the material along the stitch line, baste and then sew with your machine right along with your seam, all in one operation.

Machine Sewing: Always keep your material to the left of the presser foot of the machine, letting your left hand gently guide it under the presser foot, and your right hand helping to keep it straight as you stitch. You will find your own natural rate of speed as you become accustomed to your machine. Don't let anyone hurry you or slow you down, for you will sew the straightest and most efficiently at your own normal rate.

Seam line: When you sew material that has been basted, never sew directly on the same line, but just to the side of the basting line, a thread width away. Otherwise it will not be as easy to pull out the basting threads, and remember also to use a contrasting color for the basting.

CHAPTER 7

PRESS AS YOU GO — THE SECRET OF SUCCESSFUL SEWING

Pressing is an art. I cannot stress this too strongly, for this is what keeps your garment from having that home made look. Do not be surprised if it sometimes takes longer to press a seam than it did to stitch it. The time spent is well worth it in total effect because this is the secret of giving your work that desired professional look.

There are two kinds of pressing. First, there is construction pressing, which is the pressing done on the inside on seams, darts, and other construction details of the garment as you sew. The second type is called top pressing or finished pressing, which is usually done on the outside of the garment. Before we take up each separately, be sure to have all the things you need: a sturdy ironing board, a steam iron, a press cloth, a sleeve board, and a tailor's ham.

Construction Pressing

The cardinal rule is press as you sew. This means you must have your iron on any time you are sewing so that you will not be tempted to defer it. Every seam must be pressed before it is joined to another part of the garment. Simply press seam open with the tip of the iron and press entire seam open. Be sure to place your garment neatly on the ironing board so that you will be pressing with the grain.

It is wise to test the heat of your iron on a scrap of the fabric you are using before pressing your seams for the first time. You may find you will have problems with the material or that the iron is too hot. The advantage of a steam iron is that steam keeps from scorching your material or crinkling your material from too much heat.

Most fabrics require only a gentle pressure to eliminate the wrinkles or press seams open. But crease-resistant fabrics and tightly woven materials such as worsted require more pressure because they are made to withstand wrinkling.

You will find that certain fabrics will get a shiny look even with a steam iron, and in these cases you will need to use a press cloth. The important thing is not to drag or push the iron but to lift the iron and gently pat the material—an up and down motion.

Darts: It is best to press darts over a tailor's ham or press mitt. Press from the widest part toward the tip. For vertical darts at or under the bust or at the shoulder, press toward the center of the garment. Darts which are horizontal at the bust line should be pressed down. If there is any danger that the darts will leave a mark on the right side of the fabric, place tissue paper or brown wrapping paper between the dart and the fabric.

Seams: First press along the stitching lines, first on one side of the material and then on the other. Then lay the fabric so the seam is standing up and open and press using the tip of the iron. If there are any curved areas place them over a tailor's ham to keep the curved shape. Even if your seam is to be pressed in one direction, as for a flat felled seam, it will first need to be pressed open, to give that professional look. In such case first press the seam open, and then press it closed in the direction desired.

Hems: Press on wrong side of garment, pressing upward from the bottom fold toward the stitch line.

Sleeves: Sleeves require a sleeve board to preserve their proper shaping. After the sleeve has been attached to the bodice, press seam allowances toward the sleeve instead of opening them.

Pleats: Pleats should be pressed while still basted. Use a press cloth then remove your basting and repress to eliminate any marks of the thread.

Shirring or Gathering: Use only the tip of your iron to press into the fullness so that you do not make creases.

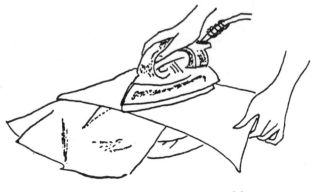

Pressing darts

Pressing Guide for Various Fabrics

Wool: Use steam iron on dry fabric on wrong side. Or use damp press cloth with regular iron set at moderate temperature. If when testing the sample the material tends to shine use a separate piece of material preferably of the same fabric, between the garment and the press cloth.

Linen and cottons: Dampen your fabric and press using high temperature. Cottons and linens nearly always looks better when pressed on the wrong side.

Synthetics: Press on wrong side using low temperature or on right side with press cloth.

Blends: Press using the guide for the most fragile of the fibers.

Rayon: Press on wrong side or on right side with press cloth using low to moderate temperature. If water leaves marks when you test your sample, place a dry press cloth under your damp cloth.

Silk: Press on wrong side. It is important to place a dry cloth between fabric and your press cloth. Use moderate temperature.

Lace and Embroidered Fabrics: Press on wrong side putting a turkish towel underneath the lace to keep the texture of the lace from matting. Press cloth is usually not necessary.

Pile fabrics: To keep pile fabrics such as velvet from flattening down, you need a protector such as needleboard. Place the cloth pile side down on the needleboard, and press on the wrong side, using a damp press cloth between the iron and the back of the fabric. If you don't have a needleboard, you can make do with a stiff clothes brush or scrub brush. Or you can stand your iron on end with a damp cloth over it to cause steam to rise, then draw wrong side of velvet gently across the covered iron.

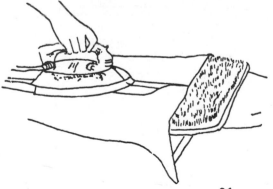

Pressing pile fabric

Tips on Pressing

1. If you are pinking your seams, do so before pressing the seam open.

2. Press with the grain of the fabric.

3. To keep pile fabrics such as velvet and corduroy from flattening down, always use a protector to keep the pile standing. For corduroy you can use a piece of the same material to make a press cloth with the pile sides facing while you press the wrong side of the corduroy press cloth. For velvet and velveteen or fleece, a needle board is best; but if you don't have one, a stiff clothes brush or scrub brush may be used. In either case place the cloth face down on the bristles, and lightly steam the wrong side. If pile fabric gets crushed down, the nap can be raised with a brush while the fabric is still steaming from the steam iron.

4. When in doubt press on the wrong side.

5. Use a gentle up and down motion lifting and patting instead of pushing or dragging the iron across the material.

6. Always use a left over piece of material to experiment on before pressing any parts of your garment.

7. To save time, a sponge can be used to dampen your fabric, if the fabric does not water spot. Instead of dipping your press cloth in water and wringing it out each time, simply keep a wet sponge handy and tap fabric lightly with it, then covering with the dry press cloth and pressing on that. To save time a sponge may also be used to dampen your press cloth.

8. To keep from having a mark where the seam is when you are pressing fabrics that mark easily, place strips of tissue paper under the edge of each seam as you press, then place a double thickness of tissue on top of the seam, dampen slightly, and press with warm iron.

9. Bias sections of a garment must always be pressed with the grain of the fabric and not on the bias. Otherwise the material will get out of shape.

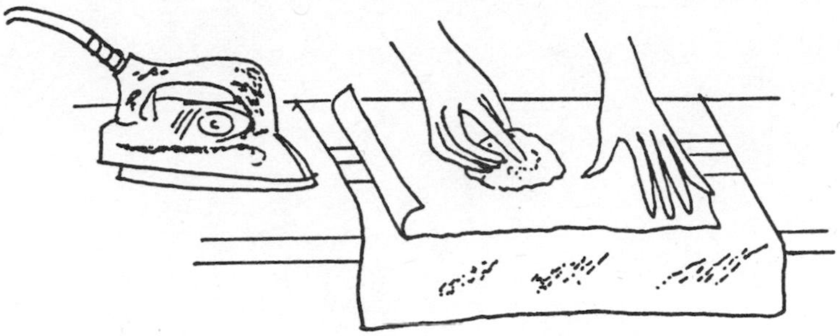

Wetting press cloth with sponge

Finished Pressing or Top Pressing

When all the sewing is done, the finished pressing or top pressing is done on the outside. If you have kept your garment on a hanger as you finish each piece and have kept from rumpling it as you work on it, this final pressing will be very easy.

For finished pressing, follow the same rules as for construction pressing. That is, press with the grain instead of on the bias, and use tailor's hams or press mitts for curved areas.

The rule is that curves should be pressed on curves, and flat areas should be pressed on the ironing board.

If your sample piece of material showed shininess when you tested it with the iron, use cheesecloth when ironing on the right side of such fabrics.

Press the parts of the garment in this order.

1. Collar
2. Sleeves
3. Shoulders
4. Facings around neckline and sleeves.
5. Front of bodice
6. Back of bodice
7. Skirt

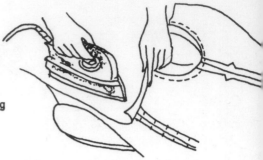

Finish pressing or top pressing

Here is a checklist of things to do before your final pressing.

Zipper: Always close it before final pressing.

Basting: Remove any remaining basting, such as in pleats.

Sleeves: Press out any creases on wrong side. Must always be pressed on sleeve board.

Hem: Press lightly on wrong side with grain of fabric before turning dress right side out.

CHAPTER 8
HOW TO MAKE A DRESS THE EASY WAY

You won't really feel a great sense of accomplishment until you've made your first dress. It's just as easy to make a dress as it is to make a blouse. So, let's be brave and make a dress, but a dress that is very simple—no sleeves, no collar, no seam at the waist.

In other words, you are going to make a shift—that is, a dress with an unfitted effect—or you are going to make a sheath. The sheath, like the shift, has no seam at the waist but is slightly fitted by means of darts to make it follow the lines of the body. A belt may be used with either one, at waist or hipline, as fashion or your taste dictates.

Now, you're ready to go. You have studied your pattern, made adjustments necessary to conform with your figure. You've cut your pattern, decided the types of seams you will use and have set up your ironing board.

You're going to put those pieces together into a beautiful work of art—your first creation.

Before you remove the pattern from each piece of material, mark it with your contrasting tailor's chalk to show whether the piece belongs to front or back—'F' for front and 'B' for back. These should of course be marked on the wrong side of the material.

Since your first dress is a shift or a sheath, you have before you a dress front, a dress back left, and a dress back right, a neck front facing, a right and left back neck facing, two armhole facings. You will also have your zipper in the same color as your garment and long enough to extend past your waist, as indicated by your pattern, usually 20 inches. Finally you will have tape for your hem, also in the same color as your dress, and a hook and eye for the back of the neck. As for the color of your thread, one shade darker than your dress is the rule.

THE 12 STEPS OF SEWING A BASIC DRESS

Before you baste any two pieces together, you must first prepare each piece separately.

1. **Staystitching:** At neckline and armholes, staystitch with the machine ½ inch from the raw edge. Stitch from the shoulder to the center of the front part of the neckline first and then turn the fabric over and stitch from the other shoulder to the center front. Do this on front and back of dress. When staystitching the armholes, stitch from shoulder to underarm seam in one operation. Staystitching prevents stretching.

Stay stitching

2. **Baste for Fitting:** Darts should be basted first. If you are making a shift, you may have only a bust dart at each side. If you are making a sheath, you will have darts at waist front and back and at bust line.

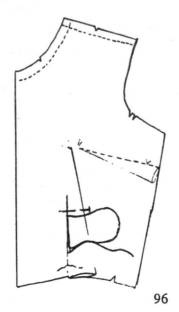

Baste for fitting

After you have basted all the darts, pin and baste together the two back pieces of your garment, sewing downward from just below the waist, where the zipper will end, to the hem. Now pin and baste the shoulder seams and side seams.

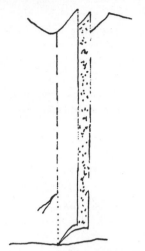

Baste for fitting

3. **Try on and Adjust:** Always remember to try your basted dress on right side out. If it doesn't fit quite right, snip basting, pin the way you want it and take off and baste again. Keep trying it on and adjusting until you are satisfied.

The order of fitting is this: Your shoulder seams serve as your anchors for any dress or blouse and should be fitted first. Next check the neckline.

Then check the bust line, releasing the dart and repinning if necessary or taking in more with pins if it was too big.

Now check the underarm seams all the way from armpit to hem making sure the waistline is the way you want it to be. At this point do not worry about the length of the skirt. That will be measured later.

4. **Final Stitching of Darts:** Now that the fit is the way you want it you are ready to machine stitch. It's easier to work with flat pieces. Simply take out the basting of the side seams and shoulder seams so that you again have a dress front and a basted dress back. To machine stitch darts, start at the widest part, and stitch to the narrowest. You can finish the darts by either back tacking one stitch at the beginning and end of the dart, or you can leave the thread long enough to tie a knot to secure it. (To back tack place

stitch regulator at proper position and turn balance wheel by hand in the right direction until your machine has taken one stitch backwards.)

5. **Insert Zipper:** First sew your center back seam leaving an opening ¾ths of an inch longer than your zipper. Sew from your opening down to the bottom of the garment. Now baste the zipper opening close along the seam line, and press the basted seam open. Place the zipper face down along the pressed open seam. Pin and baste with small stitches to hold securely in place. The end of the tape at the tab end should lie even with the edge of the neck and will extend ¾ths of an inch above the tab.

Now turn the garment to the right side, and using the zipper foot on the machine begin stitching on the left side of the zipper ¼th of an inch from the basted seam line. Continue stitching to ¼th inch beyond the end of the zipper—which you have marked with chalk—lift your presser foot to turn to stitch across the end of the zipper, turn another right angle by lifting the presser foot again and turning the material continue stitching up the other side of the zipper to the neck edge. Press and remove basting.

Inserting zipper

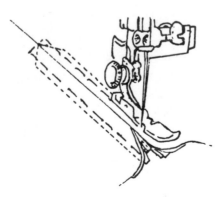

6. **Shoulder Seams:** Pin, baste and machine stitch the front and back of your dress at shoulder seams. Machine stitch from neckline to armhole. Direction of stitching is important in making garments hang properly. If the back is a fraction wider than the front at the shoulder seam, ease the back to fit the front.

Shoulder seams

7. **Neckline Facing:** First sew the back facings to the front facing, right sides together. Press seams open. Then stitch ¼ inch from the outer edge; use the stitching as your guide to turn under, press, and stitch. Now lay your dress out flat on your table, right side up. Place the facing on the neckline so the right sides are together, matching notches and the shoulder seams. Pin into place, baste and machine stitch. Before turning the facing into the dress, clip the seam allowance several places around the curve of the neckline so that it will lie flat. Be careful not to clip into the stitching. Then understitch the facing to the seam allowance so that it will lie flat and keep the facing from riding up and showing. Press facing in place and tack with a few stitches at the shoulder seam.

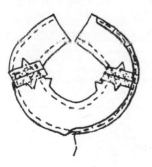

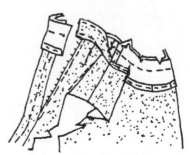

Neckline facing

8. **Armhole Facings:** Again lay the dress out flat on the table, right side up. Do the same thing with the armhole facing as you did with the neckline facing, leaving the underarm facing seam to be closed when you sew the side seams of the dress. That is with right sides together, stitch facing to armhole, matching notches, clip curve, press and understitch facing to seam allowance and press again. Turn under and stitch the outer edge of the facing.

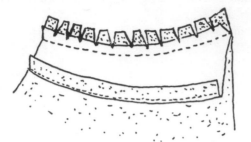

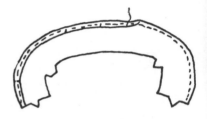

Armhole facings

9. **Side Seams:** You are now ready to join your side seams. Starting at the outer edge of the armhole facing, pin, baste, and machine stitch, sewing from the armhole facing down to the hem of the dress in one operation if it is fitted. You can sew in either direction if it is unfitted. If the dress is fitted, however, stitch from underarm down to waist; then from hem up to waist. This holds the grain in place. Press the seam open and fold down the facing, tacking it to shoulder and underarm seam. If it still needs further fastening, slip stitch all the way around the armhole. Pink the edges of the side seams, or finish in the way suitable for your fabric.

10. **Making Your Hem:** Have someone measure the length of your hem from the floor marking the line with pins or chalk. On your ironing board turn up hem and lightly press, but avoid the fold. Baste the two thicknesses together ¼ inch from the fold. Now, using your measuring gauge, measure two inches for the depth of your hem, and mark with chalk all the way around your hem. This chalk mark will be used for the guide line in stitching your seam binding on for the hemline finishing touch. The excess material is not trimmed off until after you have sewn on the seam binding. This is because it is easier to stitch when you have more material under the binding, rather than having it right on the edge. Fold the binding back and trim to within ¼ of an inch of the edge of the tape.

Marking hem

Now pin the hem in place easing in any fullness. Baste and hand sew. Use a hemming stitch or slip stitch to sew your tape to your dress.

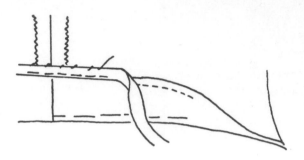

Hem basted in place with tape

Trick for marking hem by yourself: If you have no one to help you measure the hem and no automatic hem marker use this trick. Simply stand in front of a mirror with a yardstick and making sure you are holding it straight, mark a line around your hips with pins using the top of the yardstick as your guide. Now place the dress on your ironing board with the yardstick in the same position as when you were measuring and with a pin marking the spot at the other end of the yardstick. In other words, the single pin inserted into the ironing board cover represents where the floor would be. All you have to do now is measure the desired length of your hem from the single pin, turning your dress, until you have pinned it all the way around.

11. **Neckline Fastener:** As a finishing neckline touch, sew a hook and eye at the back of the neck above the tab of the zipper to hold the neckline securely closed.

12. **Final Pressing:** The sewing of your dress is complete, but according to the rules in the preceding chapter, it is not really finished until it has had the final pressing. Press first on the wrong side being sure that all seams are opened and smooth. Before press-

ing, remember to remove all basting threads. Now, turn to the right side and covering with cheesecloth for protection, give the final pressing with a steam iron.

Now your next assignment is to get different material in a different texture and color and make the some dress, with the same pattern but with slight variation. You will be surprised how much faster you go now that you know the 12 steps. You should soon be able to make this dress in two hours.

For your variations, maybe just the color and texture make the effect different enough. Or you may try adding simple patch pockets. If you add pockets, they are basted to the dress at the same time you baste the darts before checking the fit.

To make pockets, simply turn under the upper edge of the pocket and slip stitch it down, then turn under the edges of the other three sides, press and pin to the dress before basting.

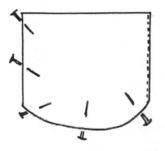

Pocket

GENERAL TIPS FOR MAKING A DRESS

1. Shortcut for Side Seams:

As you become more at ease with sewing dresses, you will be able to eliminate the basting and ripping of the side seams to check exact fit. Instead of pinning and basting the side seams on the wrong side as indicated in Points 2 and 4 of "The 12 Steps of Sewing a Basic Dress," try this short cut. Simply pin the side seams on the right side, and make any adjustment necessary by resetting the pins. Then take off the garment and mark any changes with tailor's chalk on the wrong side, take out the pins, and your garment can lie flat again for easy machine sewing.

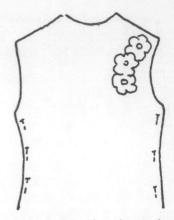

Shortcut for side seams

2. **Test for Sit-ability:** It is important to sit down in a basted garment and see how it feels and looks. Sit in front of a mirror and let the mirror be your guide. Move your arms around. Be sure that your armhole is large enough to feel comfortable because there is nothing more annoying than an armhole that binds. Always wear the same foundation garments and shoes that you will wear with the finished dress.

3. **Testing for Straight Seams:** The line from underarm to hem must hang straight. To be sure that you get a straight underarm seam line check by placing a weight on the end of a string or tape measure and letting it hang from the underarm to hem while you look in the mirror.

4. **Prevent Wrinkling:** Wrinkles make more work. To prevent wrinkling, always hang your unfinished dress on a clothes hanger when you are not working on it. It will also make sure the garment stretches as much as it is going to before hemming, particularly if it is on the bias.

5. **To Center Your Zipper:** If you have trouble making the zipper lie straight along the center back seam of your dress simply do this. Measure the width of the zipper. This is usually one inch. If it is, then measure one half inch on each side of the seam line in which your zipper is going to be inserted, and mark with tailor's chalk. Continue doing this every few inches along the seam line down to the end of the zipper opening. These marks are your guide for centering the zipper.

6. **Substitute for Basting Zipper:** A shortcut, which does away with basting your zipper is to tape it in place with cellophane tape. Place strips of cellophane across the zipper every two inches.

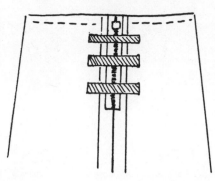

Shortcut for placement of zipper

7. If You Do Not Have a Zipper Foot: A zipper foot enables you to stitch ⅛th inch from the seam line and gives a more professional look. However, if you do not have a zipper foot for your machine you may still use your machine to insert your zipper by stitching ¼ inch from the seam line.

8. Hemline Finish. Be sure to use **seam tape** sometimes called seam binding to finish your hemline rather than **bias** tape. This gives a smoother finish and there is less chance of puckering. Be careful not to pull your hemming stitches too tight. If you do, they will show on the right side.

CHAPTER 9

HOW TO MAKE A SKIRT
How to Handle Pleats, Waistbands; and Fullness

There are many kinds of skirts—straight skirts, pleated skirts, circular skirts, bias skirts, full gathered skirts or simple A-line skirts.

Types of skirts

There are skirts made of heavier materials which are worn with blouses and sweaters for sportswear, and there are skirts made of light weight material which are part of a two piece dress.

There are lined and unlined skirts.

There are skirts with waist bands and those without. You may take your choice, whichever happens to fit you better. The important thing is to put the skirt pieces together in the proper order.

In this chapter we will take up the various skirt styles one at a time so that you may easily understand them. But all of them will follow the same order of construction. First, let's make a fitted skirt without a waistband. The steps you will follow are these.

8 STEPS FOR MAKING FITTED SKIRT WITHOUT WAISTBAND

1. Staystitching: Staystitch top edge of skirt, sewing each piece from center to hipline, then turning material over and stitching from center to other hipline. Also staystitch at least the top ten inches of hipline, sewing from bottom up. Staystitching is important any place there is danger of the material stretching while it is being worked on. Staystitching locks the grain in position.

Staystitching skirt

2. Pin and baste darts on front and back skirt. An interesting variation is to start the dart and sew it part way, letting the end of the
dart remain unstitched to form a soft pleat. If you like a tailored
effect, the darts may be stitched down on the outside. If your skirt
is of heavy material, open plain dart by cutting almost to the fold
and pressing open, then overcasting the raw edges to keep from
raveling. Press toward the center seam if darts are uncut.

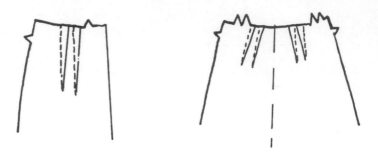

Skirt darts

3. Pin and baste front to back leaving an opening on the left side
for the zipper—usually about 8½ inches. The way to figure the
precise opening you will need is this. Measure the zipper length
from the base of the bottom-stop to the end of the turned-up pull
tab. This will probably measure 7½ inches. Then add an extra
¼ inch for extra ease and ⅝ths inch for your seam allowance.

4. Try on for fit. Check darts and waistline, taking in or letting out
if necessary. The major problem in skirt fitting is making the skirt
hang straight.

Check side seams with plumbline as mentioned at end
of previous chapter under "Testing for Good Fitting." If the seam
swings foward so that the skirt sticks out in front, correct it by
raising the back of the skirt until the side seam is straight. Then
with tailor's chalk mark a line at your natural waist, trimming ⅝ths
of an inch above this line, to leave a seam allowance. If the side
seam swings to the back making the skirt poke out in back, do
the opposite as above and raise the front of the skirt at the waistline until the side seam is straight. Again mark your natural waistline with tailor's chalk and trim ⅝ths of an inch above this line
to leave seam allowance.

Adjustment if back skirt hangs improperly

Adjustment if front skirt hangs improperly

5. Machine stitch side seams. Sew upward from hemline to waist, this prevents any slight sagging. Press open and finish edge.

6. Insert Zipper. For a side seam skirt zipper, use the one-lap method. It is called one-lap because the fabric laps over the zipper in only one direction.

Directions for One-Lap Zipper

A. Using your sewing machine's longest stitch, baste the zipper seam closed on the wrong side and press open. Unzip the zipper, and place it face down on pressed-open seam allowance.

One-lap skirt zipper

B. First, we are going to attach the tape of the zipper to the back part of the skirt. Place a pin across the bottom of the tape to hold the zipper in place against the seam allowance. Attach zipper foot to right of needle, and baste stitch tape to the seam allowance only, sewing from the bottom of the zipper to the top of the skirt's seam allowance. The teeth of the zipper will lie along the seam line, and the stitches will be in the center of the tape.

C. Zip up the zipper, shift your zipper foot to the left of the needle and adjust stitch regulator to normal stitch. We are going to put the final machine stitching on the same strip of zipper tape but closer to the zipper. To do this, take out the pin, turn back the zipper so that it is face up but still on the seam allowance. Now smooth back the material from the zipper tape so there is a narrow fold in the skirt seam allowance that is right next to the teeth of the zipper. Stitch as close to the edge of this fold as you can get, again starting at the bottom of the tape and stitching to the top of the skirt. You will be stitching through three thicknesses—the folded over seam allowance and the tape of the zipper.

D. Now we are ready to sew down the other side of the zipper which has the overlap. Your zipper is still closed. First, stitch across the bottom below the zipper, where the pin was. Turn a right angle and continue stitching upward along the other side of the zipper, again stitching closely to the zipper teeth. This time you are stitching through the tape, the seam allowance and the skirt front.

E. Press and take out seam basting, and your zipper is complete.

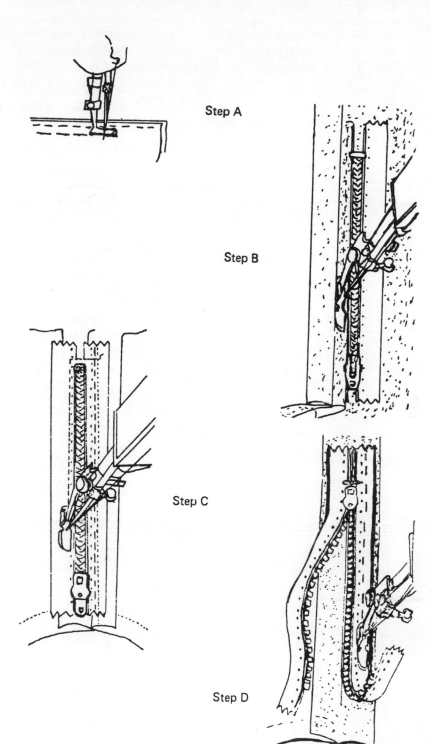

Step A

Step B

Step C

Step D

111

7. Finish Top of Skirt with Facing. If your pattern does not have a waistband, it will have a skirt facing. A skirt facing is applied much as the facing for the neckline and armhole of the dress you made in a previous chapter, so it should be easy for you. The steps for attaching the facing are these:

A. Sew back facings and front facings at side seams.

B. Overcast the under-edge of facing before attaching to skirt.

C. With right sides together, stitch facing to the waistline, being sure to match the notches and side seams.

D. Top stitch facing close to seam allowance to keep facing from rolling up .

E. Turn facing to inside, press and tack to side seams and darts.

F. Turn under ends of facing and hand stitch to zipper tape.

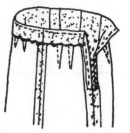

Finishing top of skirt with facing

Sew a hook and eye above the zipper to fasten the opening at top of skirt.

8. Make Hem. Follow instructions for hemming dress (given in previous chapter).

You have just made a plain straight skirt without a waistband. Now you're ready to make skirts with many variations, still following the same basic order of construction.

The lining of a skirt is an important variation. Linings are necessary to help skirts hold their shape. Skirts can have lining only in the back, or they can be fully lined. Your pattern will probably tell you the lining material that is recommended, but linings can be made of sheath lining material made just for this purpose, which carry various trade names. They can also be made of silk, cotton, or Pellon which is used mainly to stiffen.

Lining a Skirt:

A. To cut out your skirt lining follow your skirt pattern exactly as you did for your skirt, but of course leaving out the facing parts.

B. Sew your lining exactly as you did your skirt and turn inside out.

C. Finish the bottom either with a hem or by pinking.

D. Pin the lining to the skirt wrong sides facing each other. Be sure to match side seams.

E. Machine stitch lining to skirt only at waistline. The lining is attached to the skirt just before the facing is attached.

F. If you are using only a lining for the back of the skirt stitch it right along with the side seams of the skirt.

G. To finish off the lining at the zipper, turn under the seam allowance, and tack it to the side of the zipper.

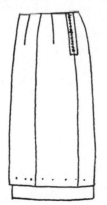

Lining a skirt

Skirt With Waistband:

The waistband is added at the same time you would have been finishing the top edge with a facing. Your waistband becomes your top finish.

Directions for Making Skirt Waistband

A. Use heavy grosgrain ribbon or tape or other interfacing material to line your waistband. This is to prevent the band from creasing when you wear it. Cut the interfacing the same length as the waistband but only half as wide. When you place it on the waistband, the seam allowance will make a border around it.

B. Catch Stitch interfacing to band on wrong side of half of the waistband.

C. Beginning at the zipper side of the skirt front, place the right side of the waistband against the right side of the skirt making sure to leave an overlap for buttons and buttonholes or hooks and eyes. Pin, baste and stitch.

D. Now fold over the waistband, and pin to the inside of the skirt. Press lightly.

E. Turn under the bottom edge of the waistline, and handstitch to the inside of the garment so the stitches will not show on the outside of the garment.

F. Sew on hooks and eyes for closure or a button if you prefer. Directions for these are in Chapter 11.

Circular Skirt (Or Gored Skirt)

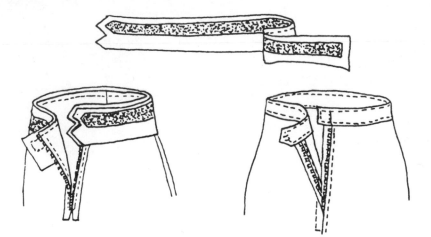

Skirt with waistband

114

A circular skirt is frequently used in children's dancing costumes, and grown-ups' square dance or skating outfits. A circular skirt may be cut in gores or in one complete circle.

There are several important differences between the handling of a slim line skirt and the circular skirt. First, if the skirt is to be lined, it is to be sewn right along with the skirt. Each section of the lining is placed over each section cf the skirt and it is pinned, basted and stitched as if it were a single thickness of material. However, if the lining is very heavy, it should be cut a little shorter than the skirt so that it ends above the top of the hem and is finished with pinking shears.

Another important thing is that a circular skirt must hang twenty-four hours before putting the hem in. This is because the bias must be allowed time to stretch to its normal condition so that when you hem it, it will not stretch any more.

Circular skirt

Pleated Skirt:

Fleats are simply folds made in the fabric to add fullness and allow ease of movement. They can be completely unstitched, or they can be stitched part way down from the waist.

115

They can be pressed or unpressed. Sometimes the edges of the pleats are stitched to give a sharp edge and keep the crease in.

There are several kinds of pleats, but no matter which you are making, remember they must always be sewn from the bottom up. This helps them hang perfectly. Stitching from top down can cause slight fullness at the end of the pleat due to the pressure of the presser foot, and thus throw the pleat out of line. Be sure to back stitch at the end of each pleat to prevent pulling apart.

Steps for Making Pleats

A. Place skirt on ironing board and following your pattern markings which have been transferred to your material. Lay in the pleats by folding where indicated. Hold in place by pinning each pleat to the ironing board pad at the top and bottom. Then continue pinning all along each pleat, pinning the edge with pins placed diagonally about an inch and a half apart. Press lightly.

B. Baste pleats while still on the ironing board, using silk thread, so they will not leave a mark.

C. Take the skirt off the board, and machine stitch the length you want for your garment, being sure to stitch from bottom of the pleat up. Leave in all the basting stitches even where you haven't machine stitched. Put back on ironing board and press, anchoring each pleat by sticking a pin in as you would a thumb tack. Use a damp cloth over the pleats when pressing, or press on wrong side. Never press pleats at bottom of skirt until after hemming.

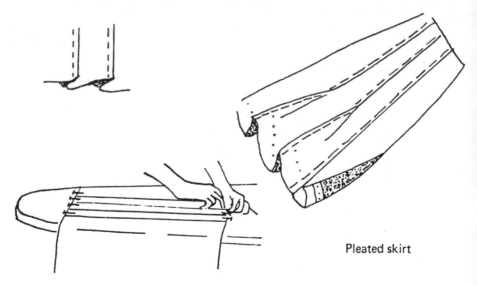

Pleated skirt

Types of Pleats

       Side or knife pleats: Pleats which are all folded to lay in the same direction.

       Box Pleats: Pleats that are made in sets of two, which are turned in opposite directions from each other and pressed down to form a panel.

       Inverted Pleats: These are the opposite of box pleats, that is the knife edges are turned to face each other. The inverted pleat is the one most frequently used at the bottom of the skirt, front or back to give room for walking.

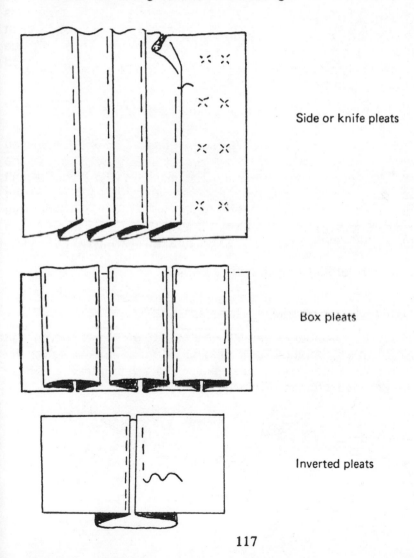

Side or knife pleats

Box pleats

Inverted pleats

Bias Skirt

A bias skirt is one which is cut on the bias rather than with the grain in order to make it cling to the figure. Because of its cut, each piece of the garment should be staystiched all the way to the hem line to keep it from stretching.

A bias skirt should hang on a hanger over night before hemming in order to make sure all the stretch has taken place. Otherwise the skirt will continue to stretch after the hemming and you will have an uneven hemline.

Full Gathered Skirt

The trick in making a full gathered skirt is to have the gathers even so that they do not bunch up in one area or another. You can do your gathering by hand using ¼ inch stitches, or shorter depending on how dainty your material is, but the best and easiest way is to use your sewing machine.

Use the longest stitch, the machine basting stitch, and loosen the upper tension one turn.

Steps for Gathered Skirt

A. Use tailor's chalk to mark three lines where you will stitch. The first line of stitching will be ⅜ths of an inch from the top of the skirt. The next row will be on the seam line or ⅝ths of an inch from the edge, and the third will be equal distance from the second line and will measure ⅞ths of an inch from the edge. This means that when the band has been put on the skirt, the bottom row of stitching will show slightly.

B. Using a heavy thread such as quilting thread on the bobbin, sew your three rows of machine basting.

C. Pull the three bobbin threads out a little at one end so you can hold them all together. Now holding all three threads, continue gently easing the material and pulling the threads until you have the right measurement for half your waist band.

Gathered skirt

D. Then do the same thing from the other end, pulling all three bobbin threads until the entire skirt is evenly gathered and the right size for your waist. The main thing is to be very gentle in handling your threads so they won't break.

CHAPTER 10
HOW TO MAKE A BLOUSE
Including Various Kinds of Sleeves and Collars

The most popular kind of blouse is currently called a shell. It is a collarless, sleeveless blouse which is worn on the outside of the skirt and comes to just about the hipline.

You already know how to make a shell because it is made exactly like the sheath you have just learned to make in Chapter 8. The main difference will be that the center back zipper is shorter and that the hemline is finished at the hip instead of at the hemline.

To hem your shell, turn up the lower edge one inch—instead of two inches for a dress hem—and finish with seam tape in exactly the same way.

The shell becomes part of a dress when it is combined with a skirt of the same material.

You might want to make your first two piece dress at this point since you have just learned how to make a skirt.

A blouse can be very simple or very complicated. A tailored shirtwaist is difficult for a beginner because it calls for flat felled seams and a tailored collar such as you find in a man's shirt. But if you look carefully you can find shirtwaist patterns that are less complicated and less tailored.

Blouses can have short sleeves and full length sleeves and a myriad of collars from Peter Pan to turtleneck. The neckline can be high or low, V-line or square and finished with a facing rather than a collar. Sleeves can be short or long, set in, or raglan. If you want to cover the shoulder bone but not make a sleeve, you can use the kimona style.

Whatever style you choose, there is a logical order in which to proceed.

In order to show these steps while actually proceeding to make an important blouse, let us make a high fashion long sleeve turtleneck blouse with no zipper but with buttons down the back.

Long sleeve turtle neck blouse

Choose a firm textured fabric of shantung or linen or any fabric that is easy to handle.

Steps For Making Back Buttoned Blouse With Collar And Sleeves

1. Staystitch neckline, shoulder line, and armholes.

   a. Staystitch ½ inch from edge along neckline from shoulder to center front on one side and from shoulder to center front on other side.

   b. Staystitch shoulders from neckline to armhole.

   c. Staystitch armhole from shoulder to under arm seam. Front and back pieces of the pattern are treated the same way.

2. Make darts in front and back segments, and press toward middle of garment.

3. Baste interfacing to wrong side of each back where buttons and

buttonholes will be. Buy a light weight interfacing material, cut in a two inch strip, and loosely catch stitch inner edge of interfacing to back along the fold line marked in your pattern. Tack at top and bottom.

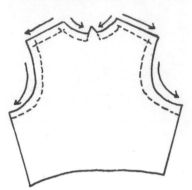

Staystitching

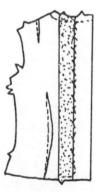

Darts and interfacing

4. Join front and back shoulder seams pinning and basting on the wrong side.

5. On the right side of the garment, pin side seams together.

6. Try on to check for fit. Check shoulder seam and side seams. Make any adjustment necessary marking with tailor's chalk after you take it off. Take out pins at side seams, and you are ready to lay your blouse flat again for easy sewing.

7. Back Opening Facings: Finish the raw edges of the right and left back facings by turning under ¼ inch and edge stitching. Then stitch facing along neckline and bottom edge of blouse right side together. Trim off interfacing that comes beyond stitch line. Finally turn facings inside, and lightly tack to the back of the blouse.

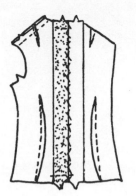
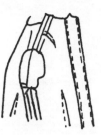
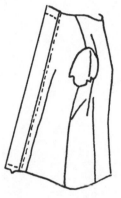

Back opening facing

8. Attach Turtle Neck Collar.

   a. Pin and baste interfacing to wrong side of collar right sides together. Fold collar, right sides together with interfacing on the outside. Stitch across ends only. Turn collar right side out, and press. To hold firm, baste close to fold.

   b. Pin baste and sew notched edge of collar to neckline of blouse, matching notches and right sides together. Finish the sewn seam by trimming off the interfacing below seam line and clipping along the curve of the seam allowance to make it lie flat without puckering. Now you are ready to attach the other edge of the collar. Turn it under and pin, baste, and hand stitch to the inside of the blouse making sure that all the raw edges are covered and the stitches do not show on the right side. The hand stitches should be just above the machine stitching on the seam allowance.

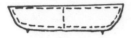

Turtle neck collar

9. Sew Shoulder and Side Seams: Finish shoulder seams first. Pin, baste and machine stitch side seams. Stitch from waist upward if loose fitting, from armhole down, if fitted. Press and pink.

10. Prepare Sleeves:

    a. Prepare cap of sleeve by stitching along seam line. Use a regular machine stitch from underarm to notch, then change to machine basting for the space between the notches. Then switch back to regular stitches from notch to underarm.

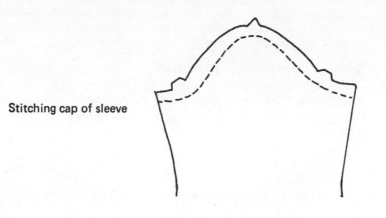

Stitching cap of sleeve

b. Pin, baste, and stitch darts on the wrong side, and press downward. Pin sleeve together, and try on.

c. Stitch sleeve seam from underarm to wrist. If the sleeve is tight at the wrist, you can leave an inch opening for a Chinese effect, or tiny zipper inserted like the one at the back of the dress. (Chapter 8)

d. Finish wrist edge of sleeve with seam binding just as you would a hem. Turn up, and hand stitch.

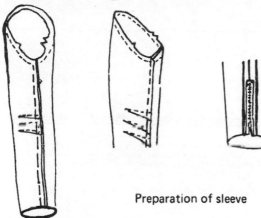

Preparation of sleeve

11. Set In Sleeve:

a. Matching notches, pin lower part of sleeve to underarm side of blouse right sides together, all along the regular size stitching which you have sewn from underarm to notches.

b. Now pull the bobbin thread of the basting stitch until the upper part of the sleeve fits the armhole, and pin in place.

c. Baste sleeve, adjusting the ease as you sew. Machine stitch. Place on sleeve board, and press, turning the seam toward the sleeve. Your iron will steam out the fullness as you press, so that there will be a smooth top to your sleeve.

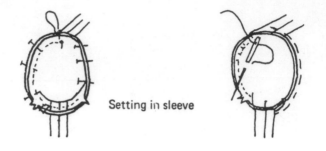

Setting in sleeve

12 Hem Blouse: Machine stitch seam binding to raw edge of right side of blouse, starting at edge of facing and continuing to other facing edge. Turn up hem as indicated in pattern. Pin and press. Slip stitch to blouse.

13. Put in Buttonholes and Sew on Buttons: There is a great variety of buttonholes you can use, such as machine butonholes, hand worked buttonholes, or bound buttonholes. For this kind of blouse I would recommend bound buttonholes.

Buttons vary greatly from tailored to jeweled. You can also make covered buttons. For instructions on buttons and buttonholes turn to the next chapter.

Sew snap fastener at neckline.

Back closing

The order that you have just learned for putting a blouse together will remain basically the same for every kind of blouse, whether the buttons are in front or back and whether the sleeves are short or long.

Now let's look at other blouse styles.

Tailored Shirtwaist Blouse

If you can make a tailored shirtwaist blouse for yourself, you can also make a man's shirt because the construction is very similar. In a shirtwaist the sleeves are not eased in, but fit precisely. The seams are flat felled throughout. The collar is edge stitched and interfaced, as are the cuffs. A shirtwaist is nearly always made with a yoke. The difference between the men's and the women's shirts is that the button and buttonhole sides are reversed. You can also use the same shirtwaist pattern but make regular seams and pink them or overcast them, depending on the material used. Made of silk chiffon or metallic fabric, a shirtwaist blouse can even be worn with an evening skirt.

Tailored shirt for men

The secret of a strictly tailored shirtwaist is very careful pressing of the seams and precise straight lines in the top stitching of the flat felled seam.

In making a tailored shirt waist people have the most trouble with the banded shirt collar, so let us take that up first in the discussion of various types of blouse collars and necklines which follows.

1. Blouse with Standing Band Shirt Collar

a. Baste your interfacing to the wrong side of the undercollar. Then, right sides together pin, baste and sew collar to undercollar on three sides, leaving the edge that is to be stitched to the neckband free.

b. Grade seam allowances by trimming the under seam allowance to ¼ inch to keep the seams from leaving a line when it is pressed. Then clip the points of the corners diagonally, again to reduce the amount of material, so that you will have a neater point when turned.

Standing band shirt collar

c. Now turn collar right side out. Press lightly, pin and baste edges, and top stitch.

d. Now, we are ready to sew the undercollar band. Again use interfacing, basting it to the wrong side of the undercollar band.

e. Put both collar bands right sides together, insert collar between them, pin, baste and stitch. Trim seam allowances so that each is of a different width, to assure flatness. Now, turn down the collar band and press.

f. You are finally ready to attach the collar band to the neckline of the shirtwaist. Pin, baste and stitch the interfaced part of the collar band to the wrong side of the shirt or blouse neckline. Again trim seam allowances to various gradations, turn seam allowance toward neckline, and press.

g. Turn under bottom edge of collar band, pin baste and top stitch to neckline, and continue sewing next to collar. Be sure that you have pulled the top band down far enough to hide the stitching underneath.

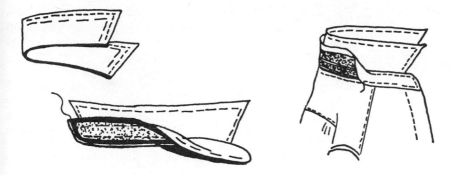

Steps for standing band shirt collar

2. Blouse with Peter Pan Collar

A Peter Pan collar is rounded to give a soft line around the face. It can be interfaced for stiffness, but for blouses you would want to use a thinner interfacing than for a tailored shirtwaist. This is cut the same size as the collar.

a. Pin, baste, and sew interfacing to the under collar on the wrong side.

b. Pin, and baste upper collar and under collar with right sides together, being sure to match notches. Stitch all along the outer edge; then trim off interfacing that comes below stitch line, and trim one of the seam allowances to avoid crease line when pressing.

c. Snip out small notches along the curved edge almost to the seam line to keep the collar from puckering when turned.

d. Turn inside out so the right side of the collar is out, and press flat. Baste outer edge to hold collar in place until it is attached to blouse. (You may also want to understitch the edge of the under-collar to the seam allowance before basting.)

e. Pin, baste, and machine stitch the under collar to the neck line of the blouse right sides together, matching notches. Trim off underfacing, and press seams toward the inside of the collar. Turn top collar down over the seam, turning under the edge, and hand stitch to the inside neckline so that no stitches show on the outside and all raw edges are covered.

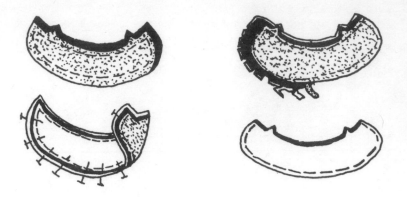

Peter Pan collar

3. Blouse with Pointed Collar

A pointed collar is made and attached exactly the way a Peter Pan collar is. The only difference is that you do not have to make little notches in the seam allowance to make the curved edge lie flat when it is turned right side out. Instead, cut diagonally across the point to remove excess material. Also be sure to make a sharp corner on each end of the collar. The trick is to take one diagonal stitch at each corner. Otherwise you may have unmatched points, or points that are not true points.

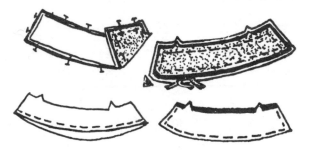

Pointed collar

4. Blouse with Decorative Facing Instead of Collar

By placing the facing on the outside of the blouse instead of the inside, you can add interesting detail. This can be finished with contrasting stitching, or several rows of stitches of the same color as the cloth. The facing can be of a different material, different color, or can be cut on the bias. Follow instructions for making a facing as given in Chapter 8, Point 7, except that the facing is attached to the outside instead of the inside.

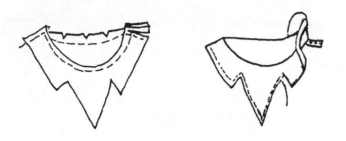

Decorative facing

5. Blouse with Plain V-Neckline

To finish off a V-neckline when you are not using a collar, simply cut a 1½ inch wide bias strip from the same material as your blouse and about 4 or 5 inches longer than the distance around your neckline—right front, left front and across back. The steps for attaching are these:

a. Starting at the point of your V, and leaving half the excess of bias strip extending below the V, pin, baste, and machine stitch bias strip to your blouse right sides together. Now in the back of the neckline, snip out several wedges to make the facing lie flat when turned.

b. Pin, baste, and stitch a seam straight down the extended ends of the bias strip where it meets at the point of the V, making sure the line conforms to the garment under it. Trim excess material, and press seam open.

131

c. Turn facing inside of garment. Understitch bias strip to seam allowance. To keep edge of facing from leaving a mark on the outside of the blouse if it is a fragile material, machine stitch the raw edge of the bias without turning it under, and lightly tack to blouse, picking up the machine thread and then picking up only one thread of the blouse at widely spaced intervals. For firmer material, turn edge under, and top stitch.

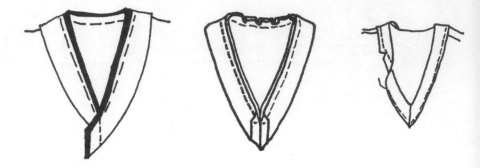

Plain V-neckline

6. Blouse with Square Neckline

To make a facing for a square neckline cut a three inch wide facing using your pattern for a guide. Make the facing on the straight grain instead of the bias. Proceed as with any facing, being sure that you raise your presser foot, and turn a very square corner. As with your V-neckline, understitch facing to seam allowance to keep it from riding up. If the blouse material is apt to show the line from the outside, treat as the bias for V-neckline, or pink.

Square neckline

132

Alternate Treatment for Square Neckline

If you do not have enough material in a single piece to make the facing described above you can make a facing from straight strips as described for the V-neckline but cutting the facing on the straight grain. Simply do this:

a. Place facing along edge of neckline right sides together and pin. Be sure that when you turn the corner the facing material is not pulled or stretched.

b. Miter the corners by folding the tape together so that it lies flat against the neckline. Baste and stitch these mitered corners; cut off excess material to make a normal seam, and press seam open. Baste and stitch facing all the way around the neckline.

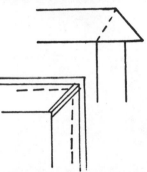

Alternate treatment for square neckline

c. Snip corners of the neckline to make a neater square, cutting diagonally across the facing and seam allowance up to the stitch line; then turn facing to the right side of the blouse, press and understitch facing to seam allowance so that it won't ride up.

d. Depending on the type of material, either turn under the raw edge of the facing and slip stitch to blouse, or if there is any danger of a ridge forming on the right side, simply stitch close to the raw edge to keep from raveling. Then pink. A third alternative is to turn edge under and top stitch. In either case, tack to the shoulder seams and in one or two other places if necessary.

7. Blouse with Yoke

Yokes are used as a decorative touch across the upper part of the blouse or as a means for giving extra fullness across the bust. Sometimes an edging or piping of contrasting material is inserted in the seamline.

Here is how to make a blouse with gathers and a yoke:

133

a. Take the bottom of the blouse, front or back which is going to have the gathers, and make two rows of machine stitching. The first is ⅜ths of an inch from the seam line, and the second is ⅝ths. Use regular machine stitching where the material is not going to be gathered, and switch to basting stitch where the gathers will be placed.

b. Lay right sides together, and pin the yoke to the bottom part of the blouse at both ends where it will not be gathered. This is only to hold the yoke in place while you pull the threads to get it to fit.

c. Pull bobbin threads until the gathers are evenly spaced and yoke and bottom fit perfectly. Pin, baste, and stitch the yoke to the lower part of the blouse. Turn yoke up, and press.

d. Top stitch on right side of yoke through both seam allowances.

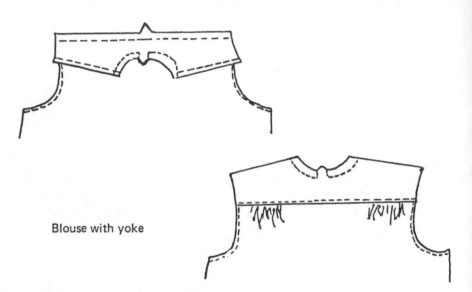

Blouse with yoke

8. Blouse with Raglan Sleeve

A raglan sleeve is often used for ease of movement. Instead of a normal shoulder line with set in sleeve, the raglan sleeve is set in starting at the neckline. They are easy to make.

a. First, prepare the sleeve. Raglan sleeves almost always have a dart where the shoulder seam would normally be. Pin, baste, and stitch this dart cutting it open almost to the tip and pressing it flat. Then stitch darts at elbow, and press down as in any other seam.

b. Leaving sleeve open flat pin. baste and stitch it to front and back of blouse being sure to match notches.

c. Snip the curve every few inches to make the seam lie flat and press seam open. Pink.

d. Now in one continuous seam, pin, baste, and sew underarm seam, starting at the waist and stitching upward through the sleeve to the wrist end. Snip several places along the curve, press seam open, and pink or finish in any other appropriate manner.

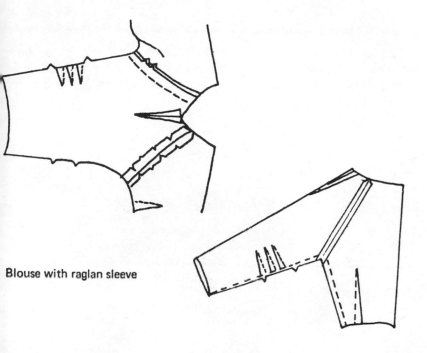

Blouse with raglan sleeve

Blouse with Kimono Sleeve

A kimono is the simplest of all sleeves to make because it is simply part of the blouse front and blouse back. No extra sleeve is required. In effect the shoulder seam is slightly rounded and extended to cover the upper arm.

a. Treat the shoulder seam as you have in making any other garments.

b. Pin, baste and stitch the underarm seam, starting at the waist and stitching to the end of the sleeve.

135

c. Now, you must reinforce the armpit area since this is where the strain will be in wearing. Take four inches of seam binding, and fold it lengthwise. Pin and baste this right along the underarm curve along the seam line. Then machine stitch the seam again stitching through this tape. This gives you a strong double stitched seam around the underarm curve. Snip seam allowance at several places at underarm curve, press open and finish seam.

You now have completed a blouse of any style you have chosen to wear with your skirt. Almost any of these blouses extended could become a dress. The shirtwaist dress is always in fashion.

Also, after you have studied Chapter 12, you will know how to make a jacket so you will have a whole suit. But before that, it is important to learn what you need to know about buttonholes and other finishing touches.

CHAPTER 11

FINISHING TOUCHES MEAN A LOT

Buttonholes, Notions, Etc.

All your fine sewing will go for naught and be wasted if your buttonholes have that "homemade" look. The wrong kind of button can cheapen it, and so can pockets that are badly set in. Snap fasteners and hooks and eyes should be firmly sewn on and be out of sight.

Belts can be another giveaway, proclaiming that an amateur was at work. All these things may sound like trivial items, but they can add up to the important touches that make or break the success of your garment. Instead of glancing briefly at this chapter, it should be one of those you study the most carefully.

Buttonholes

Before you make any kinds of buttonhole for the first time, practice making a number of them on scraps of the material that you are planning to use for your garment. This way you can work out your mistakes without disaster. Don't just stop with one practice buttonhole, but make several to feel secure in what you are doing.

There are basically two kind of buttonholes. There are worked buttonholes, which are done either by hand or machine, and there are fabric buttonholes which are commonly known as bound buttonholes.

How to determine size of buttonhole: The general rule is that the buttonhole must be ⅛th inch longer than the button as it is measured across the top. But if the button is thicker than average, you will need a slightly larger buttonhole. The best thing to do is to experiment with the size of the slit on a scrap of material. The button should slip through easily.

How to space your buttonholes: It is very easy to get one buttonhole out of line, spoiling the effect of your row of buttons, and of course spoiling the effect of the whole garment. For that reason it is important that you have a basted line on each side of your buttonholes, running from above the first button to below the last button.

Now, mark the position of each buttonhole either with a basted thread or a contrasting chalk mark. To make sure your distances are perfect between buttons, use your metal slide gauge; or if you do not have one, take a piece of cardboard and cut out wedges to mark the distance.

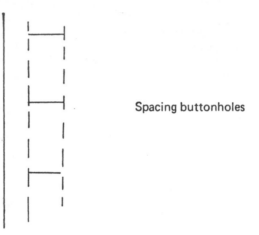

Spacing buttonholes

Bound Buttonholes

Bound buttonholes should be used whenever possible because they give your dress, suit or coat the truly professional look. However, do not use bound buttonholes on sheer fabrics, because the excess fabric would show through.

1. Prepare strips of fabric for binding your buttonhole. These should be the length of the buttonhole you have marked off plus 1 inch so you will have ½ inch extra at each end of the buttonhole. Your strip should be an inch wide on each side of your buttonhole mark. For decorative purposes you can cut this strip on the bias, but it is not recommended for beginners. Your strip should be cut so the length of the buttonholes runs with the lengthwise grain of material.

138

2. Lay the strip on your garment, right sides together, pin and carefully baste a line the exact length your buttonhole is to be. Mark
a stitch across each end to designate the width.

3. Using regular size machine stitches, stitch ⅛th inch from the
basted line on each side and across the ends, being sure your
turns are sharp.

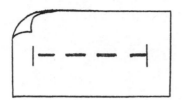

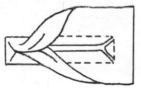

Steps for bound buttonholes

4. Using sharp pointed scissors, cut through the basted line of the
buttonhole and through both thicknesses to ¼ inch of each end.
Now make a diagonal cut to each of the four corners right up to
but not cutting into your stitch line.

5. Pull the strip through the slit you have just cut.

6. Using the tip of your steam iron, press on the wrong side along
the seam line; then fold the part of the strip that you just pulled
through carefully over the raw edge of your cut line, and press

to form a definite crease. Do this on both sides so that you now have pressed folding edges meeting in the center of the rectangle, and small inverted pleats on each end.

7. Pin the inverted pleats at each end securely in place making sure you have caught the little triangular piece so that you have a nice straight line at each end when you are looking at the right side of your buttonhole. Now, secure the ends by hand stitching, and then baste the opening of the buttonhole together with a few basting stitches.

8. If your garment has a facing, cut a slit in it exactly in the same spot as the buttonhole; then turn under the buttonhole edges of the facing, and slip stitch to the edge of the buttonhole.

9. If you do not have a facing to your garment to cover the edges of your buttonhole, use a slip stitch or other inconspicuous stitch to hold the strip in place on the wrong side, and overcast the edges to keep from ravelling.

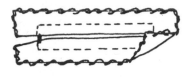

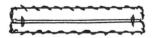

Steps for bound buttonholes

Strip Buttonholes

This is sometimes called a two-piece bound buttonhole. It is

140

a little easier to make and achieves the same purpose.

1. Prepare your strips by cutting them 1 inch wide and 1 inch longer than your buttonhole. As with the bound buttonhole, you can cut your material on the bias, however it is strongest if cut on the lengthwise grain.

2. Fold along both sides of the strip to the center so that they meet in the center and the wrong side of the material is completely hidden. Press edges.

3. Working on the right side of the garment as you did with the bound buttonhole, lay the strip along the marked line for your buttonhole, and pin at each end.

4. Baste ⅛th of an inch from the raw edges on each side of your buttonhole line; then machine stitch, leaving ends unstitched.

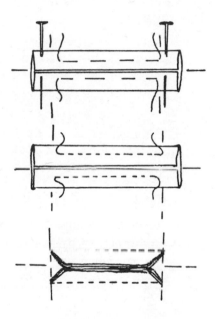

Steps for strip buttonholes

5. You now have two parallel lines of stitching to the very ends of the buttonhole. Be sure to back stitch at each end to make the lines secure. Now turn garment around to the wrong side. Using

your sharp pointed scissors, cut along the center line of your buttonhole to ¼ inch of each end. Then as you did with the bound buttonhole, cut diagonally to each of the four corners.

6. Pull the strip through the slit you have just cut.

7. Using the tip of your steam iron, press the strips in place. Then at the corners, turn the material back so that you can baste and stitch the little points to the strips. Press again.

8. Finish the same as you would a bound buttonhole either with or without a facing as described in points 8 and 9 above.

Machine Worked Buttonholes

Most people prefer machine made buttonholes to hand stitched buttonholes on blouses, lightweight dresses, and sportswear. They are stronger and less apt to pull out. Also it takes great patience and pains to make stitches as carefully by hand as a machine can make them in a hurry.

There are several ways you can work your buttonhole by machine. You can buy a buttonhole attachment for your machine which can be set for the size of your buttonhole. This attachment then automatically makes the buttonhole as you stitch.

If your machine can make a zigzag stitch, you do not need a buttonhole attachment. Simply set the dials for the width of the stitch that you want, and stitch along both sides of the buttonhole marking. Then, to secure each end of the buttonhole, set your machine so that it back tacks back and forth in the same place and seals the end shut. Cut open after stitching.

Mark your buttonholes for machine stitching just as you would for any other buttonholes. If there is a facing, they are made through both thicknesses. If there is interfacing, they are also sewn through that.

Machine-worked buttonhole

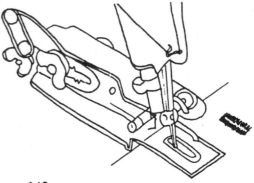

Hand-Worked Buttonholes

You will want to use hand-worked buttonholes on baby's garments or chiffon or other sheer fabric. Also, if you don't have an attachment or a zigzag stitch on your machine. There is one other place you would use a hand-worked buttonhole, and this is on a man-tailored jacket or coat—whether it is being tailored for a man or a woman—and for women's heavy coats. It is called a tailored buttonhole. The other kinds of hand-worked buttonholes are the horizontal buttonhole, which is curved around the end which gets the strain and the vertical buttonhole which is squared across both ends.

Mark hand-worked buttonholes as you would any other. The horizontal buttonholes are sewn along the cross grain of the fabric and the vertical buttonholes are made on the lengthwise grain.

Before cutting any hand-worked buttonhole run two basting rows of small stitches to mark the exact outline that your buttonhole will have, either curved at the end or straight. This also acts as reinforcement.

Tailored Buttonhole

1. Make a hole at the edge of the buttonhole that is going to receive the strain, the front edge of your garment. Use any sharp pointed scissors or an embroidery stiletto. Cut through the length of the buttonhole.

2. Overcast with a diagonal stitch around the slash you have cut, taking a few extra stitches in a fan shape around the hole you have punched at one end. The overcasting will follow the guide line of the basted rows which are used for all hand-worked buttonholes.

3. Tailored buttonholes are always reinforced with a thread product called "heavy twist" which you can buy at a tailor's shop. Run a length of this twist along the overcast edge turning the corner at the punched hole and returning to beyond the other end. The loose ends of the twist can be secured to the garment by looping them back and forth over a pin.

4. Work from right to left starting at the end away from the punched hole, and make buttonhole stitches all the way around, fanning the stitches into a half circle around the punched end of the buttonhole. The buttonhole stitch is a variation of the blanket stitch

described elsewhere in this chapter. The buttonhole stitch is made very close together so that the top edge which catches the blanket stitches and holds them in place forms a strong ridge and acts as a finish for the buttonhole.

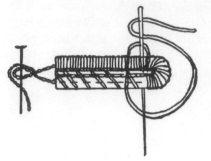

Hand-worked buttonhole

5. To finish the buttonhole at the end away from the curve make a bar tack. To do this, first take several long stitches across the end the full length of both stitch lines (3 threads will do it) and then make your tight blanket stitch over these threads with the ridge facing the buttonhole to give added strength at the end of the slash.

Horizontal Buttonholes

Make an ordinary horizontal buttonhole as you do a tailored buttonhole, except that you do not need to use the extra reinforcement of the heavy twist thread. Also you do not make a circular hole at the strain-end of the buttonhole. Simply cut along the marked line of the buttonhole using a razor blade, and putting a heavy piece of cardboard or wood underneath to protect your table surface.

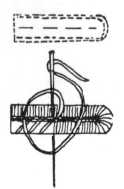
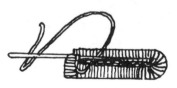

Horizontal buttonhole

144

Vertical Buttonholes

Vertical buttonholes are made just like tailored and horizontal buttonholes except that you do not have a curved end to take the strain. Instead you make a bar tack both at top and bottom of the buttonhole as explained in the tailored buttonhole, Point 5. Also, as with the horizontal buttonhole, you do not use heavy twist for any other reinforcement than your buttonhole stitches. In making buttonhole stitches by hand, you should not be able to see any fabric between the stitches. The closer together your buttonhole stitches are, the stronger your buttonhole is.

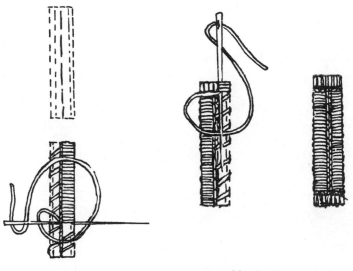

Vertical buttonhole

BUTTONS

There are basically two kinds of buttons. There are buttons pierced with either two holes or four holes for passing the thread through, and there are buttons which have a shank underneath so that the threads are hidden. The shank button can be made of metal, plastic, or other materials, such as Mother of Pearl. It can have a great variety of shapes.

The shank button is considered dressier than the button with holes through it. It is considered to be tailored when a button has holes in it.

An important variation of the shank button is the covered button. It is also called the self-covered button, because it is covered with cloth, usually of the same material as your garment or of the trimming material of the garment. You can buy a kit for making self-covered buttons, and it will have instructions which are easy to follow. You can also take buttons that you want covered to a department store or a fabric store, or a button store such as you will find in most big cities. Covered buttons are the most inconspicuous and add a professional touch to a suit or dress.

Jeweled buttons for evening wear are very elegant and almost always on a shank.

Now let's talk about how to sew on the various kinds of buttons for greatest security and for making them easy to button.

How to Mark Spot for Attaching Button

1. Final checking for the spot for the buttonhole is not made until after the buttonholes are completed. Try on garment and pin closing of garment in position with the top and bottom of the garment edge even and the buttonholes exactly where they will be when worn.

2. If the buttonhole is vertical, or if there will be no strain on the buttonhole, the button is placed in the center of the buttonhole. However as is usually the case for horizontal buttons, if there will be any strain of button against buttonhole, a button is sewn on the corner closest to the fold of the garment.

3. Mark the exact spot for the button by passing a pin in and out of the material where you want the button to be. You can then mark the spot with tailor's chalk with a contrasting color.

Marking area for attaching button

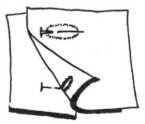

146

How to Sew Buttons with Holes in Them

1. Ordinary buttons on shirting or lightweight material: Use a fairly heavy thread doubled and knotted at the end, about 12 or 14 inches when doubled. Pass the needle from the wrong side to the right side of the material to hide the knot, and make one or two tiny stitches to secure the thread.

   Holding button so that the center of it is over the marked spot, pass the thread through one hole and down through the other several times until the button is securely held. Be sure that you leave a little ease so that it doesn't pull and is easy to button.

Sewing button with holes

2. Buttons with Thread Shank: If the material is heavy or thick, and you would have trouble buttoning it, you will need to make a thread shank under the button between the button and the garment. After making your first loop through the button eyes, place a pin on top of the button under the thread. Then continue sewing over the pin and through both eyes four or five times. Even with the pin, do not draw the thread too tightly.

   Take out the pin, and pull button as far as you can from the garment. Now bring the thread through the material but not through the button, and wind the thread around the loose stitches until there is a firm thread shank. Then pull thread through and knot on wrong side.

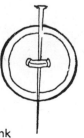

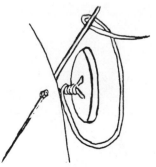

Buttons with thread shank

3. **Decorative Stitching of Buttons with 4 Holes:** By crossing the threads on top of a 4 hole button or sewing them in pairs to make a square, you can get an interesting decorative touch for a dress or suit. There is good reason for using 4 holes instead of 2 where there is strain because the area of pull is better distributed.

Decorative stitching of four hole buttons

4. **Buttons Sewn with Stay Buttons:** If there is going to be a great deal of strain on your button, use a small clear plastic button on the other side of the material to take the strain instead of letting the cloth be pulled.

Buttons with stay buttons

5. **How to Sew Buttons wtih Self Shanks:** If your material is very heavy, you can make a thread shank just as you did for buttons with holes, but usually the shank itself adds enough elevation to keep this from being necessary. The main thing is to sew the button firmly—about six times through—while keeping the thread

eased a little. Wrap the thread several times around the shank of the button before pulling it to the wrong side to knot. It is always good to make a few stitches in the body of the garment under the button before starting to sew through the holes.

The self covered buttons are sewn on like any other self shank button.

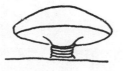

Buttons with self shank

BLANKET STITCH (also buttonhole stitch)

The blanket stitch is very versatile. When made with stitches far apart, it is decorative as well as protecting the edge of material. Sewn tightly together so that no fabric shows through, it becomes a buttonhole stitch.

Used still another way, it becomes a French tack to hold two important parts loosely joined—as your lining to your coat at the hemline.

1. To make sure all your blanket stitches start on a straight line, you may want to first draw a line with ruler and tailor's chalk at the desired distance from the edge you are sewing—½ inch or ¼ inch are standard; but don't let that influence you too much. Or you may want to baste a straight line as your guide as you do for buttonholes.

2. Work with the edge of the fabric toward you and from left to right. Knot your thread, and bring your needle through from the wrong side of the material to the right side on the marked or imaginary line you want your stitches to begin.

3. Hold the thread down with your left thumb as you take another stitch, but this time from the right side of the material to the wrong side, and also on the same level, and at the distance apart you want all your stitches to be (¼ inch is standard).

4. Bring needle through so that it passes above the thread, thus causing a loop to form at the edge of the material.

5. Continue bringing the needle through from the right side of the material to the wrong side, bringing the needle and thread in front of the loop you make at the edge of the fabric so that it catches and holds it in a fairly firm line. In effect, you will have a straight line of thread along the edge you are decorating or protecting, and a box effect.

By staggering the length of the stitches, you can make decorative effects.

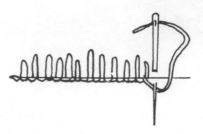

Blanket stitch (also buttonhole stitch)

BUTTONHOLE STITCH

The main difference between a blanket stitch and a buttonhole stitch is that the buttonhole stitch is so tightly sewn that no fabric shows between the stitches and a firm ridge is formed along the raw edge, to protect it. The buttonhole stitch is sewn from right to left, with the edge of the material away from you, starting at the inner end of the buttonhole. If it is horizontal, work toward the curved end which will get the stress of the button. Bring the needle through from the wrong side of the material each time, along the marked straight line.

FRENCH TACK

A French tack is an easy way to hold two pieces of material loosely together, as at the bottom of the lining of a coat, attaching it to the inside of the coat at each side seam.

To make a French tack. first take three or four stitches between the two pieces of material at the point where you want them held together. In the case of a lining, it should be held about ½ inch from the coat. Over this loose rod of stitches, make a row of blanket stitches, close together, the full length of the exposed threads, so that you form a firm link between the two garments.

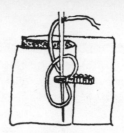

French tack

POCKETS

Pockets give an interesting accent to a dress or suit and are of two kinds—patch pockets and set-in pockets. Neither should give you any trouble. Some people avoid set-in pockets, thinking they must by very difficult, but if you can make a bound buttonhole, you can make a set-in pocket.

Patch Pockets: Patch pockets can be placed with the grain as well as at interesting angles. The main thing is to get both pockets in exactly the same position. It is wise to run a basted thread on your garment where the top of the pocket will be.

1. Prepare patch pocket by turning under top edge ¼ inch and edge stitching. Then fold the top edge to the proper depth—one inch or more—right sides together, so the raw edge of the stitched top is visible.

2. Pin to hold in place, and then machine stitch to hold in place continuing to stitch all along the seam line on the three sides.

3. Snip upper corners, trim seam allowance, and turn top hem inside out. Press before and after turning.

4. Baste under edges of pocket, and pin and baste in position on garment. Bottom corners are mitered to lie flat.

5. Top stitch to garment. If you like, you can reinforce the top corners with a second parallel row of stitches.

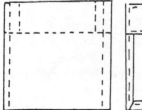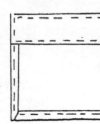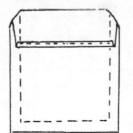

Steps for
patch pockets

Round Patch Pocket: Make this like you did the square cornered plain patch pocket, but instead of cutting the bottom corners horizontally to miter them, cut notches into the curved edge to make it lie flat.

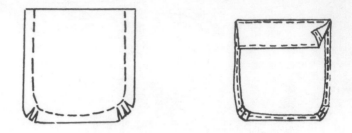

Round patch pocket

Set-In Pocket:

1. Your pattern will show you the exact position of the opening of your pocket, but if it is something you are adding to your garment yourself, mark the line on the right side of your garment. Basting the guide line is best.

2. Next, baste the piece of fabric you are using for the pocket to the garment, right sides together and placed so that the section above the line for the pocket opening is one inch longer than the bottom section.
   If you do not have a pattern for guide, cut your piece of fabric double the depth of the pocket, plus one inch and the width of the pocket opening plus one inch allowance.

3. Now stitch ⅛th or ¼th inch from the basted marking on both sides, and close the ends with stitches to form a rectangle.

4. Just as you do for a bound buttonhole, cut through the basting line, making diagonal cuts at the ends to each corner but being careful not to cut through stitch line.

5. Turn inside out, so pocket is on wrong side, press, and turn seams away from opening. You now have tiny inverted pleats at each end on the wrong side. Pin in place and baste around the opening. The lips of the pocket will touch on the center of the opening. Catch stitch them together for perfect fit.

152

6. Machine stitch on the right side close to the binding.

7. Make a pouch on the inside, pin and sew the two loose sections together, trimming edge and finishing edges with pinking shears or overcasting.

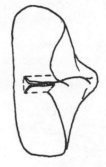

Steps for set-in pocket

BELTS

Belts come and go in the fashion picture, and sometimes they hug the hips and sometimes the waist. And sometimes they don't hug at all, but are worn very loosely. The use will help you decide whether you need a belt with stiffening or without.

Belt Without Stiffening

1. If you do not have a pattern, cut the belt about 6 inches longer than the part of your body where the belt will rest—waist or hips, and 2½ to 4 inches wide.

2. Fold along the center line, and pin and baste the length of the raw edge but leaving about 5 inches at center back for turning inside out. Also pin and baste each end, one of which you must cut to a point. Press.

3. Final stitch and turn inside out, slip stitching the place you left open. Press. If you like you can top stitch the edge or run lines of stitching to give a very slight stiffening.

4. Attach buckle with or without prong. If it has a prong, you will need to make eyelets for the prong to pass through.

Belt without stiffening

Attaching Bar Buckle

Fold the non-pointed end of the belt, and slip over the middle bar of the buckle, and hem so that it holds firmly. Sew on snap fasteners near the pointed end, being careful that no stitches show on top of belt. Directions for sewing snap fasteners are in this chapter.

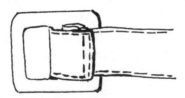

Attaching bar buckle

Attaching Prong Buckle

Fold non-pointed end of the belt and punch hole with embroidery stiletto in center of the fold. Use buttonhole or blanket stitches, or simply overcast around the hole to keep it from tearing. Slip prong of middle bar into the hole, and hem edge firmly in place.

154

Now you need holes at the pointed end of the belt to pass the prong through when you are wearing the belt. You can make eyelet holes as you did for the prong. Or you can buy an eyelet belt punch and metal eyelets at a notions counter or button shop. In either case, make first hole 1½ to 2 inches from point and several others (4 is standard) about an inch apart.

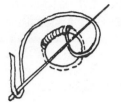 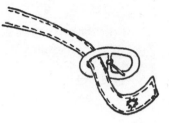

Attaching prong buckle

Belt with Ribbon Backing

The simplest way to add a little stiffening to a belt is to simply back it with grosgrain ribbon.

1. Cut belt ¾ inch wider than the grosgrain ribbon you are using. Cut the belt 7 inches longer than the body measurement where belt will sit, and make the ribbon one inch shorter than the fabric. Cut triangle points on both ribbon and fabric.

2. Place the fabric flat along the ironing board, and press under both lengthwise edges ⅜ inch, continuing around pointed end, after mitering corner, and also after snipping to make a neat turn at point where the lengthwise edge becomes diagonal.

3. Place ribbon on top to hide the raw edges and pin in place. Baste.

4. Top stitch fabric to ribbon.

5. Attach buckle, and make eyelets as directed for belt without stiffening.

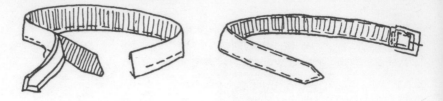

Belt with ribbon backing

Belt With Stiffening

1. If you do not have a pattern, cut the belt about 6 inches longer than the measurement of the body where the belt will rest—waist or hips—and ¾ inches wider than the interfacing. At one end cut triangular point. The interfacing can be made of stiff belt backing or firm interfacing material.

2. Pin interfacing to belt on wrong side and fold edges over it. Press, pin, baste, and edge stitch on the machine, to hold the three layers together.

3. For lining, use ribbon or the same material as the belt but about ¼ inch narrower than interfacing. Pin, baste, and catch stitch all the way around to make a tiny hem.

4. Attach buckle, and make eyelets as directed for belt without stiffening.

SNAP FASTENERS

Snap fasteners are used to hold two parts of a garment opening together when there is not much strain. The advantage of snaps over hooks and eyes is that the snap fasteners are more flat and inconspicuous.

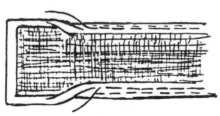

Belt with stiffening

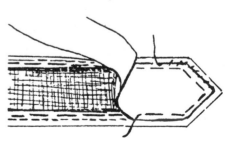

156

1. The ball part is sewn on first so it will be on top and will fit into the socket under it. Mark the place for the ball on the inside of the garment which will lap over the other.

2. Make several buttonhole or blanket stitches through each of the four holes in the snap ball, being careful not to let your stitches go through the top layer of your garment. Sew it only to the facing. Anchor with hidden stitches or knot.

3. To mark the place for the socket part of the snap fastener, rub tailor s chalk on the ball, using a contrasting color to your fabric. Then press opening closed, exactly as garment will be worn. Now you can see where the ball must fit.

4. Sew socket in place, but it doesn't matter if stitches show through since they will be on inside of garment.

HOOKS AND EYES

Hooks and eyes are stronger than snap fasteners in that they can take a lot of strain. The disadvantages are that they are not as flat and may show themselves if they are not set back far enough.

1. The hook part is sewn on first, and like the ball of the snap fastener, is attached to the underside of the part of the garment which will lap over the other part. Looking at inside of garment, the hook goes to the right, the eye to the left. If your edges overlap, use a straight eye; if they only meet, use the round eye type. Sew hook so that its edge is ⅛th inch from the edge of the garment. Use the blanket or buttonhole stitch all around the hole and a few stitches up each neck. Then anchor head of hook by taking several stitches at the top of the neck in the bend. Be sure your stitches do not show on the top of your garment.

2. Mark place for eye by pressing opening closed and taking a tiny pin stitch exactly where you want the hook to touch the eye.

3. Sew eye in place by holding it so that the pin is your guide.

Hooks and eyes

DECORATING WITH SEQUINS AND BEADS

Exciting effects can be achieved with just a few beads or sequins which cost little but add an expensive look to evening clothes.

Sequins with Bead Centers (Individual sequins)

1. First mark the design or line you want to follow on the right side of the material with tailor's chalk.

2. To apply sequins singly, bring needle through material from wrong side to right side, through the hole of a sequin.

3. String a tiny bead, usually of the same color as the sequin, over the needle next and pull the needle back down through the sequin hole so that the bead, which overlaps the sequin hole, holds it in place. You can get brilliant color effects with two tones or contrasting beads and sequins.

4. Secure stitch in underside with another tiny stitch that is hidden by the sequin before sewing on your next sequin, or make knot if they are widely spaced.

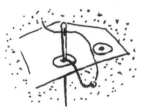

Sequins with bead centers

Sequins Without Bead Centers (Sewn in a row)

1. To fasten a row of sequins without using beads, you must overlap them. First mark your pattern on right side of garment with tailor's chalk or pin on a printed pattern on tissue paper which you can tear off after you have done your sewing.

2. Sew sequins by back-stitching them, that is, bringing needle through from wrong side of garment to the right side and through the eye of the sequin, then putting needle back down through the material at the edge of the sequin to the right and bringing it out again at the left edge. Your sequins will thus overlap to hide the stitching, but not as elegantly as the bead does. You can control the overlapping by the length of your stitches.

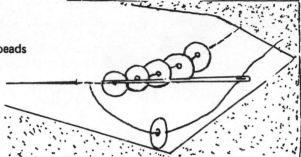

Sequins without beads

Sewing Beads

1. The important thing is to wax your thread with bee's wax to prevent getting it snarled while sewing the beads in place one at a time. Simply pull thread along the wax you can buy at a notions counter or button store.

2. Sew each bead individually using a back stitch to make them lie side by side with the thread line through them running horizontally. Bring the needle up from the underside of the material, string the bead, lay it on its side, bring the needle back through the material at the end of it, to the right. Then bring the needle back up in front of the bead, to the left, and string your next bead.

It is also possible to buy designs of beads and sequins already backed, and these can be slip stitched to your garment, saving time. but not having quite the elegant look of individually sewn beads and sequins.

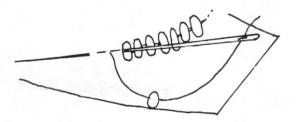

CHAPTER 12

TAILORING — HOW TO LINE A COAT OR SUIT

One of the biggest thrills you will ever get in sewing is the moment when you finish your first suit. It may be a tailored suit for day in and day out wear. It may be a soft dressmaker suit for luncheons and club meetings. It may even be a very dressy theatre suit made of elegant brocade.

Whichever you decide upon, you are half way there because you have already learned how to make and line a skirt in Chapter 9. But the top half of the suit—the jacket—is the more complicated.

However, if you use the same care you have been exercising in your workmanship and in pressing very carefully, every seam and dart as you go, you will end up with a perfectly professional job.

As you check your pattern, you will see that you will need several things you did not use in making a dress or skirt. You will need, for example, a string of weights or individual weights to make your jacket hang properly. You may also need to go to the trouble of taking the fabric to a cleaner or tailor to have the fabric preshrunk on their steam press. This also applies to the lining which will make the suit pucker around the edges if it is not also preshrunk. If you look you can find both suiting and lining that is already preshrunk.

You will find that interfacing is a very important part of the tailored suit. I recommend that you use a lightweight hair canvas for your interfacing. It is made of wool and goat hair. A second choice is woven cotton interfacing, but if you can't find these, use Pellon or any of the many new interfacings that you will find in all fabric stores today.

Choice of Fabric

The tailored suit looks best in such materials as worsted, wool gabardine, tweeds, flannels or corduroys.

The dressmaker suit gives a softer appearance, and therefore the fabric you choose should be of a lighter weight or softer—faille, velveteen, bengaline, or a loosely woven wool. Do not attempt to make a suit with crepe material, however, until you have made several others because it is too thin and soft to handle easily.

Besides brocade for a theatre suit you can use Chinese satin, peau de soie, or velvet.

Cutting Out Your Suit

You have already learned the proper steps in cutting a garment, marking all your directions on the fabric, so all you will need to do that is different is cutting your lining and interfacing. There is only one thing you will need to do in marking your suit material, however, that you have not found necessary before, and that is to mark the grain lines and center front and backs.

Cutting the Interfacing

Try to make sure your pattern has extra pieces for the interfacing. But if it does not, use the collar and front and back pieces of your jacket pattern for your guide. The front interfacing is cut exactly like your front except it ends three inches below the armhole curving slightly upward toward the bust and then curving down to the waistline. The piece down the front should be about 4 or 5 inches wide.

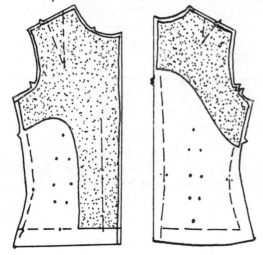

Interfacing

161

The back interfacing covers the upper 5 inches of the back up to the neckline and curves down to a point 3 inches below the armhole where it meets the front interfacing.

Cutting the Lining

If you do not have separate pattern pieces for your lining, cut the front lining piece to within ½ inch from the front facing line. Cut the back lining with an extra 2 or 3 inches allowance at center back so that you can make a pleat for ease.

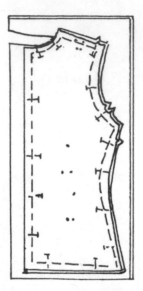

Cutting the lining

STEPS IN TAILORING A JACKET

1. **Stay stitching:** Stay stitch all raw edges of your jacket material ½ inch from the edge, including sleeves.

2. **Pin and baste** all darts, front and back, shoulder and side seams.

3. **Prepare sleeves:** Tailored jackets quite frequently have a two piece sleeve. Working with the smaller piece on top of the larger one, match notches and pin, easing the fullness of the larger piece over the elbow. Match notches of front and back of sleeve at underarm seam, pin and baste. Press lightly. Pin and baste sleeve to jacket armhole.

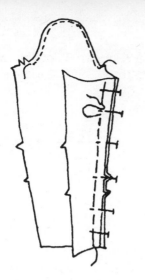

Sleeves

4. **Pin and baste undercollar** along neckline.

5. **Try on jacket for fit:** Put on garment right side out over foundation garment and blouse you will be wearing. Be sure not to fit jacket snugly, for you must allow room for lining and interfacing. Also be sure to pin the jacket properly in front so that the center front of one side matches perfectly the center front of the other.

Top of sleeve should fall along natural shoulder line and elbow ease should be directly over elbow. If you are tempted to make sleeve tighter, try bending your arm to be sure you have plenty of room.

Mark for sleeve length. Check fit of collar to be sure it hugs the neck and rolls smoothly. Check position of buttonholes. If you make any changes or corrections in darts or seams, rebaste and try on again before continuing.

6. **Final Stitching:** When you are sure that everything fits as it should, you are ready to final stitch all darts and main seams and press open. If darts are too heavy, cut open to eliminate bulkiness, and press flat. If not, press toward center front and back, and snip in to center of dart to keep from pulling.

As you are sewing remember to press as you sew, and never final stitch anything that has not been pressed. In making suits, press on wrong side of garment using damp press cloth.

Be sure to use a tailor's ham or other padded cushion to press all seams.

7. **Prepare Interfacing:** If you have had to make any alterations in your pattern, be sure to make the same alterations in your interfacing.

a. Prepare your darts in a different way from usual to eliminate bulkiness. Instead of sewing them, slash them through the center fold, and lap one over the other to where the stitching line would have been. Pin and baste together. Trim close to seam.

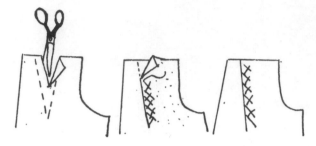

Interfacing darts

b. Lap shoulder seam and underarm seam the same way you did the darts, machine stitching or catch stitching the pieces together at shoulder and underarm.

c. Now pin interfacing to wrong side of jacket, pinning and basting along front and neckline edges and armholes.

Pinning interfacing to wrong side of jacket

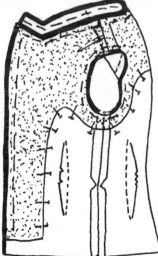

d. To hold interfacing surface in place, use padding stitches to tack to front lapel facing. The padding stitches are simply diagonal basting stitches as described in Chapter 6. To keep the stitches from showing, pick up only one thread from the jacket fabric, and use the same color as your jacket. While you are making these padding stitches hold the lapel over your hand to make it roll the way it should do when finished.

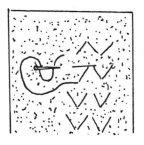

Padding stitches

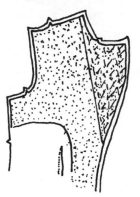

Jacket lapel with padding stitches

e. Trim off the front edge of the interfacing along the seam line so that when the facing is turned the seam will not be too thick.

f. Beginning at front bottom edge of jacket, pin and baste ¼ inch twill tape all the way up to the end of the facing along the seam line and then slip stitching it on both sides so that one side is on the seam line and the other catches the interfacing. This step is important because it keeps the roll of your lapel in perfect place.

Sewing twill tape to interfacing

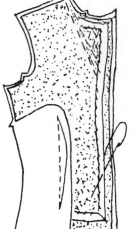

165

PREPARE PARTS OF THE COLLAR

8. **Final stitch undercollar:** Remove undercollar from jacket where it has been basted. Machine stitch back seam of undercollar. Press open.

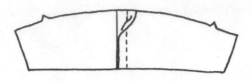

Final stitch undercollar

9. **Now do the same with the interfacing,** except you lap the seams and use padding stitches to attach to undercollar. This will form the roll of the collar.

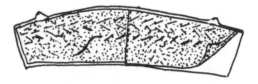

Final stitch undercollar interfacing

10. **Undercollar to jacket:** Now you are ready to attach the undercollar to the jacket permanently. Pin, baste, and machine stitch under-collar to jacket right sides together, being careful to match notches. Snip out seam allowance of interfacing up to the seam line, and then clip seam allowance at close intervals along neck line to allow it to lay flat. Press seam open, using your tailor's ham to shape as your press.

11. **Attach Upper Collar to Facings:** Pin, baste, and stitch upper or top collar to the front facings, right sides together, matching notches. Press seam open.

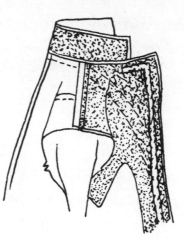

Sewing undercollar to jacket

Attaching upper collar to facing

12. **Pin and baste the facings and collar** which you have just prepared to the front of the jacket and undercollar, right sides together, matching notches.

Since outer facing is slightly larger, ease upper collar to under, and upper lapel to lower lapel. This gives a fine roll to the collar and lapel.

13. **Now machine stitch facings to jacket** beginning at the hemline of center front and stitching up to the center back of collar. Then stop, and start stitching other side the same way.

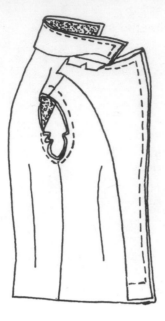

Baste facings and collar

14. **Trim out interfacing in seam allowance** close to stitching. Trim one seam to make it narrower than the other. Now clip diagonally across corners of lapels, collar, and hem.

Trimming interfacing

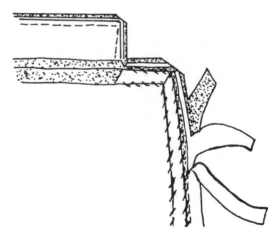

15. **Turn facings to inside** (In order to get a crisp edge to your garment, always press seams open before turning.) Baste along edge of the collar and facings to keep seam from showing and anchor in place. Press on outside very carefully.

168

16. **Make bound buttonholes** as directed in Chapter 11.

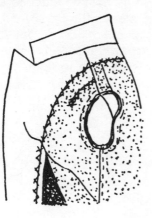

Catch stitch facing to interfacing

17. **Catch stitch facing to interfacing,** and finish the back of bound buttonholes.

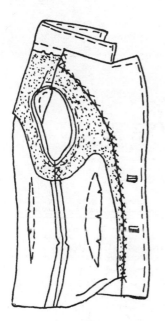

Jacket with finished bound buttonholes

18. **Final Stitching of Sleeves:** Machine stitch all seams in the sleeve. Press open. Run two rows of machine basting stitches across cap of sleeve, and pull gently until the sleeve fits the armhole. Secure the threads to lock fullness into position. Press out fullness on a sleeve mitt. Then set sleeve into armhole. Pin, baste and sew. Check again to make sure length of sleeve is right.

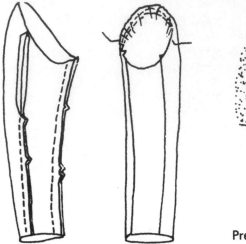

Preparation of sleeve

Check length of sleeve

19. **Interfacing for Hem and Sleeve:** Turn up and pin the hem of the jacket and sleeve at the length that is right for you, and trim off excess leaving a hem of 2 inches in depth for the jacket and a little less for the sleeve. Now press shrink the hems with steam iron until they lie perfectly flat.

Then cut strip of interfacing on the bias, making it ½ inch wider than each hem. Insert this strip in the hem of the jacket and the sleeve slip stitching the lower edge to the fold of the hem and the upper edge to the inside of the jacket. It is important to pick up only one thread in the body of the jacket and to use the proper thread so the stitches won't show.

20. **Inserting Weights at Hem of Jacket:** Weights are used only at the hem of the jacket and not at the sleeve. Lay a string of small weights, which you can buy already prepared at a notions counter, along the fold of the hem so that it is covered when the hem is turned up. Tack in place. If you do not have string weights, use individual weights which you can cover with lining material, and tack to the side seams and the center back seam, if there is one, so that they are hidden inside the hem.

21. **Hemming:** Catch stitch raw hem edges of sleeve and jacket to the interfacing. Continue catch stitching the rest of the facing making corners neat.

22. **Final Pressing Before Lining:** Now is the time to press the whole jacket thoroughly with a steam iron. If possible take it to a tailoring shop to have it professionally done.

23. **Lining:** The worst thing you can do is end up with a lining that is too small. That is why the lining is cut larger in the back than your jacket pattern, to make sure there will be extra fullness inside. It is always better to have a lining that is a tiny bit larger than to have it even a tiny bit too small. If it is too small, it will pucker up your jacket so it will not lie right, and you will have no ease of movement.

Therefore, if you have made alterations in your jacket and are transferring them also to the lining, be sure not to make too drastic changes in the lining, if you are making it smaller. Also it bears repeating that if your lining material is not of the preshrunk type, you must preshrink it or have it done by your dry cleaner.

a. Side Seams and Waistline Darts: Pin, baste and final stitch only the darts at the waist line and the side seams. Snip in several places along dart and the side seams near and on the waistline. Press darts toward center front and center back, and press side seams open.

b. Shoulder Darts: Instead of making regular darts, simply lap it over to the stitchline, and catch stitch with the right side of the material facing you.

c. Back of Lining Pleat: At the center of the back collar line, make the pleat—just a single knife pleat—and catch stitch at the top for about 2 inches. Now catch stitch the pleat for another 2 inches at the waistline.

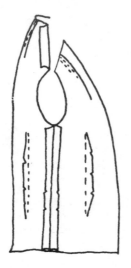
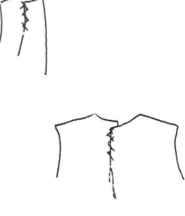

Preparation of jacket lining

d. Pin Lining in Position: Use a padded hanger or a dress form to hang your jacket on wrong side out, in order to fit your lining to it easily. The lining is right side out as you place it on the jacket, wrong sides together. First match the center back seams and notches. Then pin in position along the front along the neckline and around the armhole. Place your pins at right angles to the seam lines.

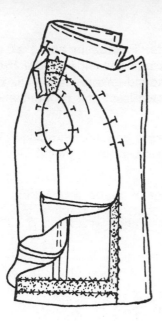

Pinning lining into position

e. Secure Side Seams: Lift lining so that you can pin the side seams of the lining to the side seams of the suit. Baste the seam allowances together under each arm from armhole to a point of about 3 inches from the hem.

f. Secure at Shoulder: Your shoulder seam still has not been made, nor will it be in the usual way. Instead turn under the raw edge of the back shoulder, and lap it over the front shoulder edge which you must tack to the shoulder seam allowance of the jacket. Slip stitch back to front along the seam line.

g. Secure Back of Neck: Now turn under the seam allowance at the back of the neck, nipping the seam allowance in several places to make it lie flat. Slip stitch from shoulder seam to shoulder seam.

h. Tack Lining to Armhole: You have not yet inserted your sleeve lining. But right now is the best time to baste the body of your lining to the seam allowance of your jacket all the way around the armholes.

i. Secure Front of Lining: Now that you have anchored all upper parts of your lining, you are ready to make a neat finish at the front edge of the lining. Turn under the seam allowance from shoulder line to a point about 3 inches from the hem and pin in place. Slip stitch.

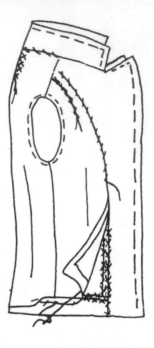

Securing lining to jacket

j. Hemming Lining to Jacket: Turn under the hemline of the jacket lining and pin in place over the hem of the jacket so that ½ inch to an inch of the jacket is left showing. In order to have a little ease in the body of the jacket—top to bottom—fold back the lining as you slip stitch, and place your stitch line about ½ inch from the folded edge. Now your jacket will not draw in movement. Now finish slip stitching the corner which you left undone when you sewed the front.

k. Prepare Sleeve Lining: The sleeves are the last step in putting in your lining. First stitch your seams just as you did in making your jacket, pressing seams open and making running stitches along the cap of the sleeve to hold in the fullness. Now pull the jacket sleeve through the armhole, and slide the lining sleeve over the jacket sleeve wrong sides together. Match notches and seam lines, and pin in place.

174

l. Secure Sleeve Lining: Turn under the sleeve lining, and lap it over the seam allowance of the main body of the jacket around the armhole. Pin and slip stitch in place at seam line.

Finally pin, baste, and slip stitch the hem of the sleeve lining, turning it under the same way, and attaching it to the hem of the jacket sleeve so that ½ inch of your jacket sleeve shows.

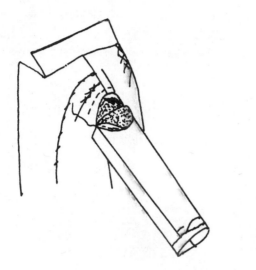

Sleeve lining

24. **Sew On Buttons:** The selection of your buttons is very important to your suit. A very tailored suit will have bone buttons of a matching color. A dressmaker suit may have covered buttons, or metal or self shank buttons as fashion or your desire dictates.

For your elegant theatre suit, covered buttons are appropriate as are jeweled buttons.

You will find complete directions for sewing these on in Chapter 11.

25. **Press Jacket and Lining**

STEPS IN TAILORING A COAT

If you can make a jacket, you can make a coat. You can make a winter coat, a spring coat, or an evening coat.

The same steps are followed all the way except for a few points which I will give you now. For a winter coat, you will need to know a few things about adding a warm interlining. The only important difference is the matter of hemming.

How to Hem a Coat and Lining:

1. Let coat hang twenty four hours before inserting your lining and measuring hem. This will assure that its weight will have stretched out as much as it is going to stretch.

2. Mark the hem of your coat, and finish with seam binding as you learned in hemming a dress.

3. Hem lining separately either turning under raw edge or finishing with seam binding. Make lining ¾ths of an inch to 1 inch shorter than your coat.

4. The hem of the lining faces inward against the hem of the coat.

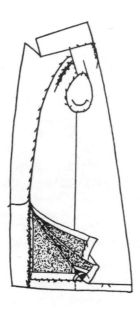

Hem and lining of coat

5. At each of the side seams, at the top of the hem make a 1 inch long French tack to hold the lining loosely to the coat for ease of movement. Directions for this are in Chapter 11.

How to Interline a Coat

1. Cutting Interlining: An interlining is cut just like a lining except that you do not need the pleat at the center back and you cut the hemline just to the length of the lining so that it rests in the fold, when you hem the lining. Some people prefer the interlining to go only to the hip and this is optional.

   Your interlining will resemble outing flannel and is made of wool. If you do not want to go the trouble of making a separate interlining, you can buy a material called "Sunback" so that your lining and interlining are combined in one material. "Sunback" is satin on one side with a flannel backing. A thinner lining-interlining combination is "Milium," which is simply a satin lining with aluminum backing which seals in the heat.

2. Trim Seam Allowance: Cut off the seam allowance all along the front of the interlining and around the back of the neck.

3. Darts: Treat your darts as you did for your interfacing, slashing them through the center and lapping one over the other to the seam line. Catch stitch together.

4. Shoulder and Underarm Seams: To eliminate bulk, treat all seams as you did the darts, lapping together, one over the other and basting together, or machine stitching through the center.

5. Attach Interlining to Body of Coat: Turn your coat inside out, except for the sleeve which remains hanging on the inside, and hang from padded hanger, or on a dress form.

   Pin interlining to coat at shoulders, along side seams, and around neck, and down front.

6. Pin and baste armhole of interfacing to seam allowance of coat and tack side seams to seam allowance of coat.

7. Just as you would do with a lining, catch stitch interlining to facing of coat around the back of the neck and continuing down both front facings to a point about 3 inches from the hemline.

8. Prepare Sleeve Interlining: Trim away seam allowance at top and bottom of sleeve and down each side. This is to avoid bulkiness in the seams. If your sleeve is cut in two or three sections, only use interlining for the outside arm section and

not under the arm. Catch stitch interlining to the sleeve lining all the way around to secure, and then sew underarm seam by machine.

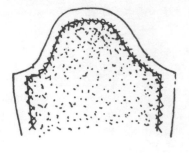

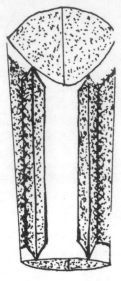

Sleeve interlining

9. Attaching Sleeve Interlining to Coat Sleeve. Pull sleeve of coat through armhole so that it can be worked on wrong side out. Pull sleeve interlining over sleeve, and attach to sleeve just as you learned to do with the lining, lapping the sleeve interfacing over the body of the coat around the armhole and catch stitch in place.

Attaching sleeve interlining

10. Finish Front Lower Corners: You have left the lower front corners of your interlining free to fit it into the lining. The lining is fitted over the interlining as described earlier in the chapter. When you get to the hemming of the lining, simply fold the lining over the interlining, and hem the lining to the interlining. Then catch stitch tne 3 inches which you have left undone.

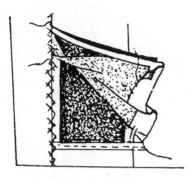

Finishing coat lower corners

CHAPTER 13
HOW TO ALTER READY MADE CLOTHES

Do you have clothes in your closet that you are not wearing simply because they don't fit? They're too short or too long, too short-waisted or long-waisted, too big or too little in the hips or waist or bustline. Or too wide in the shoulders or baggy in the seat, or you name it. The correction you need to make is as individual as you.

Everyone, almost without exception, has a measurement which does not coincide with the standard measurements used by the pattern makers. You may be size 12, and your neighbor may be a size 12, and yet your figures do not look quite alike.

Your figure is as individual as your face. You may have unused clothes hanging in your closet that could make you the best dressed woman on your street.

Let us take the problems you may have one at a time, by the area of the garment, and see what to do about it.

How to Lengthen a Skirt or Dress: The first thing you have to do is check to see whether the old crease will show if you lengthen your dress or skirt. To do this, take out the old hem, and press with a damp cloth and steam iron on the wrong side.

If your crease comes out easily when you press the garment, you can lengthen the skirt up to an inch simply by turning up at the proper length and rehemming.

However, if you need to lengthen your dress the full length or almost the full length of your hem, you will need to make a false hem.

How to Make a False Hem:

1. Use material of the same weight or slightly lighter than your garment (but never heavier) and cut it in 2½ inch strips.

2. If it is a straight skirt, cut the material with the grain; but if it is a flared skirt, cut on the bias.

3. Place the strip against the bottom edge of the skirt right sides together, and pin, baste, and machine stitch.

4. Turn false hem up, measure 2 inches, mark, sew on tape along marked line to finish hem, trimming off excess under tape.

   Make sure that none of the false hem material shows on the right side. When possible have a little border of your garment material turned up also.

5. Check length again to make sure it has been lengthened enough before doing your final stitching. Press before and after hemming.

If the crease remains, or if you still don't have enough material to make your dress long enough, you can still lengthen it using one of several methods.

1. Lengthen garment to the desired degree, and then place braid of narrow or wider width—whichever looks better—and in a blending or contrasting color to suit your style and height. A taller slimmer person can wear a contrasting color better than a shorter or a stouter person who needs an unbroken color line.

2. You can put the hem back in as it was and cut about 5 inches from the hemline all the way around to make an inset of contrasting or blending material. A lace inset is lovely in an afternoon or cocktail dress. You can also find material that has an overall embroidered effect.

3. You can give your dress a tunic effect by shortening the skirt still further and making a new slimmer skirt bottom which you attach at the stitch line of the folded under hem. To integrate the new material in the overall look, make a facing of the same material for the neckline of your dress.

4. If it is a two piece dress or suit, you can lengthen your skirt by adding a yoke at the top of the skirt where it will be hidden by an overblouse or jacket. In order to do this, take off the band and let out the side seams and darts so the skirt will drop down over the fullest part of your hips. Use a skirt pattern as your guide in cutting the yoke which is actually a new top to the skirt but made in material as closely matched to your skirt as possible.

If you do not have thread of the proper color, simply take out the thread from the old hem, and save it to make your new hem.

How to Shorten a Skirt or Dress: This is the simplest alteration of all unless your dress has special problems such as pleats or knitted material.

If there is no special problem, mark and hem just as you would in making your garment after first, of course, taking out the old hem. If your hem line was irregular so that putting it up slightly makes it wider in spots, take off the seam binding, which may be re-used if in good condition, and re-mark the width of your hem. The ideal width of a hem is 2 inches.

If this is thin or slippery material, pin and baste close to the fold line at the bottom of the garment to secure before measuring and trimming of the excess material. Then mark the width of the hem with tailor's chalk, machine stitch the seam tape on the chalk mark, cut off the excess material under the tape, and hem to the garment.

To Shorten Pleated Skirts: Treat skirt as if you are making it for the first time, except that now you must rip out the original hem and any top stitching along the lower edge of the pleats, and press. Use the ironing board to reset pleats and to be sure you have an even hemline, as described in the chapter "How to Make a Skirt".

To Shorten Knits: If you have a dress which was knitted for you but is now too long, it is still possible to shorten it without unraveling it. The trick is to secure the knitted threads before cutting off the excess material. First measure and mark the length of the skirt as you want it to be. Now measure 2 additional inches, marking that line with tailor's chalk with contrasting color. Now machine stitch along the chalk line with a zig-zag stitch so you will have a little give or elasticity. Trim off excess material close to the stitch line, and use catch stitch or cross stitch along the raw edge to hem to the garment. If you try to use seam tape on the edge, there will be no give to your hem. Your hem line must be flexible.

Refitting Skirt and Side Seams

How to Take in Skirt: Always mark your ready-made garments for alterations by putting them on right side out. This is because both sides of the body are not alike. For example, one hip may be higher or differently shaped from the other. Pin the side seams

182

the way they should be. Then take off the garment, and mark with contrasting color tailor's chalk on the wrong side before taking out the pins. If there is too great a change, you will now rip out the side seams, and re-baste along the chalk line, and then re-fit before stitching on the machine.

If your skirt is too large through the waist, you will need to rip off the waist band and refit through the darts at the waist so you will not have to take out the zipper. Then put the waistband back on as described in Chapter 9.

new darts   old darts

Refitting darts if skirt waist is too large

How to Let Out Skirt: If your skirt is too tight in the side seams, check the amount you have available to let out in your side seams. You may also find excess width by letting out the darts or changing the darts to tucks so that they are only caught at the waistline. In French construction you often see tucks instead of darts to give a softer effect. Here are the steps.

1. Rip out old seams.

2. Press out creases on wrong side with steam iron.

old darts   new darts

Refitting darts if skirt waist is too small

3. Baste in new seam line, and try on to check fit.

4. Final stitch. If your seams are too narrow, protect them by slipping folded bias tape over them and sewing each seam allowance separately.

If your skirt is too tight in the waistline and just letting out your darts is not enough, you will have to resort to more drastic measures.

How to Let Out Waistband on Skirt:

1. Rip off waistband of skirt.

2. Release darts as much as needed, changing to tucks if necessary.

3. If additional material is needed, you may have to remove zipper and use part of seam allowance to give you additional width. You may need to sew on tape or piece of the same material to give you the needed seam allowance for resetting your zipper.

4. If your waistband is too small, you may have to add a piece of material as close to the same color and weight as possible on the end where the button is. The buttonhole end will cover it.

How to Correct a Fold Below Waistline: If your skirt has a fold or is bulging below the waistline, eliminate it by taking off the back or front of the skirt band above the bulge and raising the skirt so that it fits smoothly across your hip line. Try on, and with a piece of tailor's chalk, mark a line at your natural waistline. Unless there is a great deal of excess this should just be eased up into the waistline or waistband. However, cut off excess before adding waistband, if necessary.

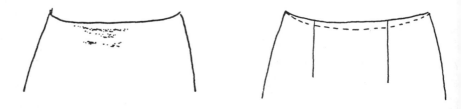

How to correct a fold below skirt waistline

184

How to Correct Crooked Side Seams:

1. For a skirt: If your skirt's side seams sway to the front, follow the above instructions, as if there were a fold below the back waistband. It it sways to the back, lift the front at the waistline. You can check whether a seam is straight by tying a weight at the end of a string or tape measure and holding it under your arm at the beginning of the side seam line.

2. For a Full Length Garment: If the seam sways to the front, correct it by making a bust dart in front to lift it under the arm until it hangs straight. For this you will have to rip both side seams from the hem to the dart area. After you have sewn back the side seams, you will need to readjust your hem, cutting off some of the back, or lengthening the front, whichever looks best on you.

   If the sway is to the back, there is probably too much fullness in the front panel. Rip upward from hem to as far as necessary to take out some of the fullness of the front at the lower side seam. Pin and baste to be sure the garment hangs properly before final stitching.

REFITTING TOP OF DRESS OR BODICE

How to Take in Side Seams of Bodice: If a blouse or bodice is simply too big for you, do the following:

1. Have someone pin the side seams for you under the arms, on the right side. Take off, and mark with tailor's chalk of contrasting color before taking out pins.

2. If it is a sleeveless top, you will need to rip the facing where It crosses the seam line so you can make it fit the garment as before.

3. Check to see whether you have enough room in your armhole. If not, trim out excess material until you have enough freedom. To be safe, you can make a pattern with tissue paper before pinning your side seams which can be your guide on how much to cut your armhole. Remember to allow ⅝ths inch for seam allowance.

4. If you have sleeves, you will need to rip out the under part of the sleeve at the armpit. If you take ½ inch out of the bodice. you must take the same amount out of the sleeve at the armhole.

185

How to Let Out Side Seams of Bodice: If your blouse or bodice is too small in the side seams, make sure that the color has not become so faded that the material that is let out in the seams makes it hopeless. But if the color is uniform when you have ripped out the seams and pressed them, proceed in the same way you did in the side seams of the skirt:

1. Baste in new seam line, and try on for fit.

2. If you still need a little additional looseness around the waist or under bust, release the darts if there are any.

3. Final Stitch. If your seams are too narrow, widen the seam allowances and protect them by slipping folded bias tape over the edge of each one separately and stitching on the machine.

How to Correct Placement of Darts: Darts which come up from the waistline should never come over the crown or highest point of the bust. Side bust darts should point toward the crown of the bust but never cross it.

The most frequent problem is that the darts are too high.

If Bust Darts are Too High or Low: Rip out side seams and place darts so they correspond with your bust line. If you have a heavy bust, it may look better to have two small darts instead of one large one.

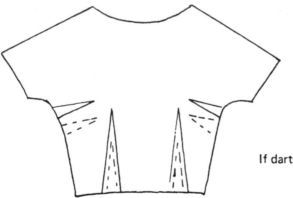

If darts are too high or too low

If Waistline Darts are Too Fitted: To get rid of a too-tight look under the bust, release the darts, and make several small tucks instead or eliminate them completely. Also if you are low busted, darts only emphasize this and it's better to have tucks.

186

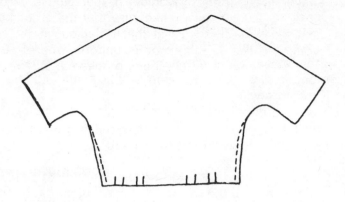

Releasing waist darts

How to Get Rid of Blousiness: (Shortwaisted)

If there is excess fullness above the waistline in front or in back, such as in a shirtwaist dress, rip the waistline seam, and remark the line of your natural waist on the right side of your bodice. Then re-attach to skirt, and try on before final stitching. Cut off excess material at the bottom of the bodice if needed.

It may also be that you are short waisted and that is why there is excess material in your bodice. It would be simpler to buy clothes that are made for the short waisted person.

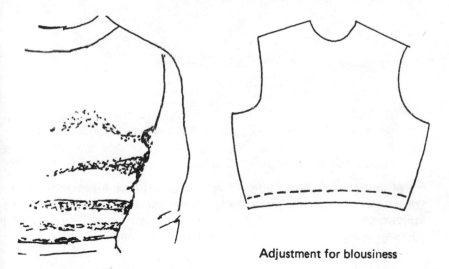

Adjustment for blousiness

187

How to Alter a Dress if You are Long Waisted:

If you are long waisted, the seam line of your dress often shows above your belt. The first thing you can do is let down the bodice seam at waist line as much as possible. You may have to protect your bodice waistline seam with seam binding if this makes it too narrow.

A second thing you can do, and a much simpler thing, is wear a wide belt of similar material or leather or even of big metal links if your figure is not too petite.

How to Correct Shoulder Lines: If the shoulder line of a sleeveless dress falls too far to the front at the shoulder bone, rip the shoulder seam, and lift the bodice front slipping it under the back shoulder seam until it forms a straight line from one inch behind earlobe to the tip of the shoulder bone. Cut off excess back shoulder seam. You will have to take off the facing of the sleeve and reset it.

If your garment has a sleeve, rip out the sleeve all across the top and follow the same procedure for straightening the shoulder seam. Stitch across the top of sleeve with machine basting stitch, and pull the bobbin thread until the sleeve again fits the armhole.

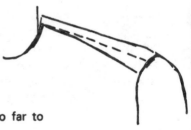

Adjustment for shoulder seam falling too far to
the front

If Shoulder Seam Sags to Back: If the shoulder line of a sleeveless dress falls too far to the back at the shoulder bone, do the opposite, as above, and raise the back of the bodice, cutting off the excess in the front shoulder seam.

If Shoulders are Too Wide: If your shoulders are too wide, open shoulder seams, and make darts in front and back tapering to fit. Slash open, press and clip corners to make them lie flat where the seams join shoulder seam.

If one or two narrow darts don't do the job, then it is better to take the sleeve out and recut the bodice using a pattern which you know fits you. The top of the sleeve will also have to be readjusted or recut.

Adjustment for shoulder seams

that are too wide

Alternate of above adjustment

How to Get Rid of a Fold at Back of Neck: If your bodice bunches right under the collar in the back, it will be necessary to take off the collar and to rip out both shoulder seams. Then, using a pattern which you know fits you, re-mark the shoulder and neckline, and cut off the excess. The problem is not in your collar but in your bodice, for there is too much material from waistline to neckline Simply resew garment and collar, as you would in making a new garment.

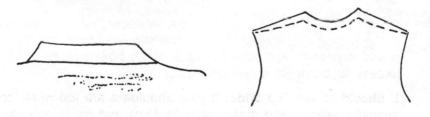

Adjustment for fold at the back of the neck

189

How to Get Rid of Fullness Above Bustline: This is a problem that seldom happens, but it might if you are particularly flat chested. The simplest thing to do is to wear a padded bra with this garment, or you can follow the instructions above except that you will recut the shoulder and neckline at the front of the dress to get rid of the excess material at the bust.

How to Correct Necklines: The most common problem is bagginess at the neckline. If it is a rounded neckline without collar, you can usually run a machine basting line in the seam line after taking off the facing and pulling the bobbin thread gently all the way around until it lies flat. Take in the facing at the shoulder to conform. The neck fullness should then be gently steam pressed out as you did in making the cap of a sleeve.

If your dress has a collar and it is too baggy to be attractive, you will need to take off the collar, take small tucks until the neck fits, and then reset the collar.

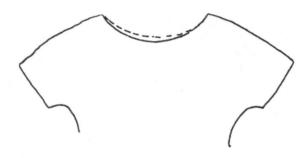

Correcting bagginess at the neckline

You may also consider getting rid of the collar completely by recutting the top of the dress with a collarless neckline that looks good on you.

CHAPTER 14

MONEY SAVING ARTS
MENDING, DARNING, PATCHING, ETC.

Have you ever thrown away a favorite dress simply because you had burned a cigarette hole in it, or it was starting to show through at the elbows? The fact that it may have been starting to show wear is proof that it was a favorite. It will really take very little time and effort to put it back in wearing order.

It is a great challenge to make something old or damaged into something as good as new—to extend its life another season. More than that, it is a great challenge to see how much money you can save by learning the womanly arts of mending, darning, patching, turning of collars and other clothing repairing.

About that cigarette hole, for example, you can do one of two things. Depending on the material and size of the hole, you can either reweave it—darning, that is called—or you can take a little piece from the hem and insert that, patching.

Actually you should take a few hours of your time to go through your entire wardrobe, including your underwear, and make a list of every thing that needs something. Set these garments aside, and as you learn what can be done, and have practiced on scraps of material, make your final graduation test the repair of your own wardrobe— top to bottom, from your evening skirt that has a hole where your heel went through it in dancing to your bra strap that is about to pull loose and your half slip seam that is frayed.

If you handle the clothes for all your family, it would really pay you to get a large mending box and keep it well stocked so that any moment you have time to simply sit and fix a few things, you have all your supplies handy.

Whenever you make a garment or shorten a ready-made, save

the scraps against the day the garment needs repair. Keep them in your mending box or near it.

Stocking Your Mending Box

Single-edge razor blades for ripping

Fine embroidery scissors

Pins

Magnifying glass on a stand for reweaving

A stocking darning ball

A steel crochet hook, fine size to pull threads through

Darning needles and blunt-end tapestry needles if you are going to darn woolens and sweaters and heavy knits

Embroidery hoops if you are going to do machine darning

Thread: Fine thread for darning — #150 cotton for darning lace and fine fabrics, and #100-120 for machine darning. Cotton and nylon darning yarn for light weight knits and yarn for mending sweaters or heavy socks.

Mending liquid or rubber cement if you are going to repair lace or net.

Scotch-tape to hold patches in place while working on them.

These are the special things you will need, but it is also good to keep extras, whenever you can, of hooks and eyes, snap fasteners, buttons of assorted sizes, elastic the same size as your undergarment and bra backs, pieces of net, and other thin materials which you can use for strengthening thin spots in a garment. If you repair men's work clothes or children's clothes, you may also want to keep on hand press-on tape for holding rips or patches in place.

MENDING

Mending is anything you do to repair a garment, or to reinforce a weak spot. The important thing is to know which stitch to use in which place. You have already learned the various kinds of stitches earlier in the book.

Hemming Repairs: Go over hems of all your clothes and use whichever hemming stitch is needed. Use plain hemming stitches if it just needs to be held in place, slip stitches if you don't want stitches to show on top of your garment, catch stitching for knits or heavy fabrics where raw edges cannot be turned under, and overhanding where strength and invisibility are important, such as patching or reattaching lace to your dress or slip.

Ripped Seams: For repairing machine stitched seams by hand, use the back-stitch to fill in the gaps between the machine stitchings and overlap into the original stitching for added strength.

Frayed Seam Edges (Seam Allowance):

If your seam allowances are fraying so threads hang down on the inside of your garment, use the overcast stitch along the raw or pinked edge to keep from weakening your seams.

Pulled Seams or Stretched Seams: If the seam line itself needs reinforcement because it has been strained or stretched so much that the threads show on the right side of the garment, use the slip stitch on the right side along the seam line.

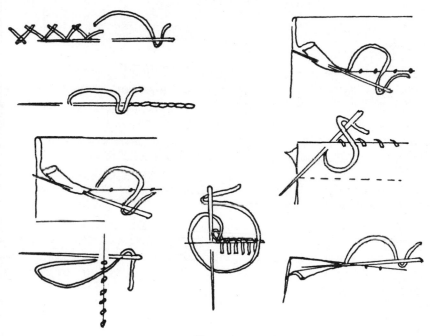

Hemming repairs

Weak Places in Garment: Sometimes just taking long running stitches on the inside of the garment, using thread the same color and texture as your garment, strengthens the material sufficiently to lengthen the life of the garment. Simply take running stitches in rows back and forth over the weak spot, catching only one or two threads on the right side. The long stitches are always underneath.

Frayed Edges and Corners: Use a blanket stitch making very shallow stitches to protect an edge that is fraying and to reinforce weakened corners such as on pockets. Use very tiny stitches on clothing, and larger ones in making household repairs such as on towels and table linens.

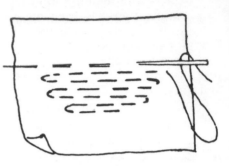

Repairing weak places in garment

Frayed Buttonholes: Use the buttonhole stitch to reinforce or repair machine made buttonholes as well as hand worked ones. You can give a bargain basement garment a more expensive look and a longer life by reworking the buttonholes by hand right on top of the machine stitching.

DARNING

Darning is the technique used to add new threads to fill in where needed, to fill in small holes, to repairs tears, and to reinforce spots that have worn thin.

It is important to study the weave of the fabric and make your garment resemble it as closely as possible. For this your magnifying glass on a stand is needed.

Another important thing is to use thread which resembles the thread of the fabric in size, color, and texture. Perhaps you have a piece of the material which you can pull threads from, or ravel along one edge of the seam allowance or hem. Or you may be able to find exactly what you need at a thread or yarn counter by taking your garment along to match. For darning cottons, find the appropriately colored fine cotton thread. For woolens or knits, find darning wool or darning cotton in the right color and texture. For fine silks and rayons, simply take silk thread of the right color, and unwind it so that you can take one ply of it to thread through your needle. Silk thread is made of two ply or two tiny threads rolled together.

How to Darn a Small Hole:

1. Snip off any ragged edges or burnt edges of the hole.

2. Starting about ¼ of an inch back from the hole, run little stitches in rows up and down in straight lines to the edge of the hole, taking a long stitch across the hole, and continuing the line about ¼ inch above the hole. The lines should be as close together as the threads of the material you are reweaving and should not end in too perfect a line or they will be noticeable—so vary the lengths of the lines slightly. Work on right side of the material so the darn will be more inconspicuous.

3. After you have all your lengthwise threads in place so that the hole and surrounding material are covered or filled in, do the same working back and forth across the hole. But this time as you come to the long threads that cross the hole vertically, weave your needle and thread over and under the vertical threads in a horizontal direction and back into the surrounding fabric. Follow the design of the material so that if necessary you will take up two threads at one time in a staggered pattern. Be sure that you never pull your threads too tightly and that all the threads lie flat. But on the other hand, do not leave excess length in the threads across your hole or the darn will have puffiness.

   There will not be many threads to cut off because you've simply turned a corner to change your direction. But whatever ends there are should be cut off on the wrong side, leaving a little loose end to keep it from unraveling. All the raw edges of the hole should be covered on the right side and visible only on the wrong side.

4. Steam press on wrong side. Then brush with a stiff clothes brush on right side if it is on woolen material or other napped fabric.

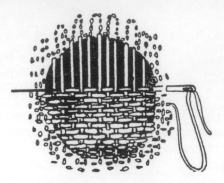

Darning a small hole

If the Material is a Knit:

1. Straighten lines of the tear by cutting horizontally above and below the hole and raveling out the material in between.

2. Run a thread through the loops across the top and across the bottom to prevent any additional raveling from taking place.

3. Now, as you did for a plain darn, run lengthwise threads up and down from upper loop to lower loop, joining them together in an almost vertical line.

4. Now, run your crosswise threads so that each stitch makes a little loop around the vertical lines which anchor in the loops below. Work from right to left starting at the bottom of the hole and making rows one above the other until the whole area is filled in.

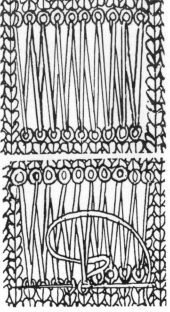

Repairing knitted
fabrics

196

How to Darn a Tear:

1. Place the area with the rip or torn place face down with the edges held together, and place a piece of scotch tape or other transparent tape across it to hold it together along both edges. This will be removed when you are finished.

   There are some materials that are too thin or easily raveled for sticky tape, so use instead a piece of net or other thin material of the same color, and baste your torn edges to that, right at the edge of the tear.

2. Turn material over on right side, and make little running lines, as inconspicuous as possible up and down in different length rows across the tear, from one side of the tear to the other.

3. Tear off tape or trim off excess net, and steam press on wrong side.

   If the tear is a straight line, you will only need to go once across, meandering up and down and up and down in a continuous zigzag line from one end to the other. But if the tear is on the bias, you will need to follow the grain, and make vertical lines and then horizontal lines as you did in darning holes.

   If the tear forms a corner or right angle, you will go up and down and up and down one time in each direction, and the two rows of stitches will overlap at the corner of the tear reinforcing it.

Darning a tear

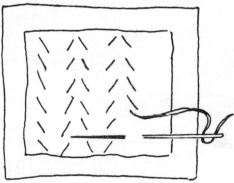

How to Darn with your Sewing Machine: Machine darning should only be used on work clothes, children's play clothes, and household linens that are used for every day. You cannot make machine darning look inconspicuous. But you can make a very strong darn.

197

1. Loosen the screw on top of the machine until it is so loose that the presser bar lifter no longer lifts the presser foot. You may have to lower the feed dog so it won't grip the material too tightly. Set machine to a short stitch.

2. Use thin material of the same color as your backing for under the hole, or weak area which needs darning. Baste this to the wrong side.

3. Place the two thicknesses together in your embroidery hoop to hold it tight, and slip it under your presser foot.

4. Start the machine slowly, and moving the hoop back and forth, let the machine stitch back and forth across the hole in both directions until the hole is filled in or the weak area is strengthened. Just as you did in hand darning, make the rows of various lengths so they will not be too conspicuous.

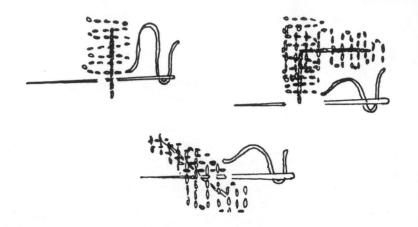

Darning on the sewing machine

PATCHING

Patches are pieces of material inserted rather than a reweaving of material. Even though there is no hole, sometimes a patch is used as reinforcement to keep material from showing through at worn spots such as elbows and the seat of a skirt or trousers. This is a very valuable trick in greatly extending the life of a garment.

You do not always have to sew the patch in place. You can buy press-on tape to hold the patch to the material. For children's and work clothes there are also ready made patches which can be pressed to knees and elbows right on the right side which give added strength and wear to the garment. There has even been a fad for wearing patches on the elbows of men's and women's sweaters in interesting contrasting materials.

Patch to Reinforce Worn Places:

1. Using net or other thin material of the same color, baste a large enough piece of material to cover the worn place on the wrong side.

2. Now that the reinforcement material is held in place, make padding stitches up and down on the wrong side of the material making sure you catch only one thread on the right side of the garment. Steam press on wrong side.

Patch to reinforce worn spots

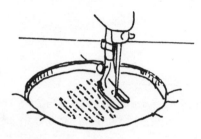

How to Make a Hemmed Patch: A hemmed patch should be used on work clothes and other places where it doesn't matter if it shows a little. If your material is knitted, cut the hole which needs patching into a round shape. Otherwise cut a square or rectangle, making as small a hole as required to remove the damaged area and straighten out the lines.

1. Place a piece of material you are using for patching underneath the hole that needs the patch, right side up, so that both right sides are facing you; pin in place. The patch should be about an inch larger than the hole on each side for easy working.

2. Clip diagonally into the corners of the hole about ¼ inch, press under and baste. Still on the right side, hem the ironed edge by hand with a slip stitch to make it inconspicuous, or top stitch on the machine if it doesn't matter.

199

3. Turn over to the wrong side, and finish back of patch by trimming raw edges to about ½ inch, and turning under.

4. Baste and catch patch to wrong side with slip stitch if it needs to be less visible, or sewing machine if it doesn't matter.

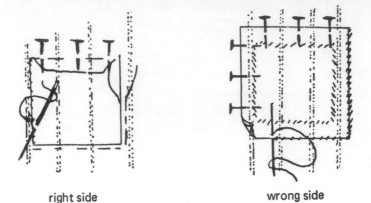

right side   wrong side

Hemmed patch

How to Make an Inset Patch: The inset patch is valuable because it is almost invisible and can be used where you must match the design. It is important, however, to use this only on firm materials such as silks and rayons that will be dry cleaned and won't be subject to strain.

1. Cut the smallest square or rectangle possible to get rid of the damaged place, making sure that you are cutting with the grain.

2. Clip diagonally into corners of the rectangular hole ¼ inch deep, and turn under and press.

3. Cut a patch exactly the same size as the hole plus the seam allowance, and place it exactly over the hole so that the right side of the patch exactly fits into the hole, and the clipped seam allowances exactly match on the wrong side of the garment.

4. Pin or baste the seam allowances to hold the patch precisely in place.

5. Slip stitch on the right side catching the edges of the patch to the edges of the hole.

200

6. Now on the inside of the garment turn both patch seam allowances toward you and the garment away from you so that a ridge is formed and overhand stitch along the edge with very small stitches to further secure the patch in place.

7. Overcast seam allowance edges to finish, and press them open for a truly invisible patch. (It is possible to machine stitch the patch, but it is very hard to do a perfect job.)

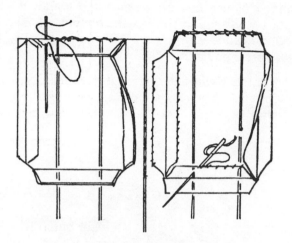

Inset patch

How to Make a Fitted Patch: This is an easier patch, and it is cut so that it will fit without seams. It is good for firmly woven materials and heavy materials. It can be treated like a tear and darned in by hand along its edges. It can also be anchored with press-on tape.

1. Steam press the damaged part of the fabric to shrink out fullness even before you cut the hole into a rectangle or square.

2. Make your patch the exact size of the hole, cutting with the grain just as your rectangular hole is cut.

3. Baste twice across the patch and hole to hold it in place in one direction, and then baste two times across the patch and into the material in the other direction. You are now ready to lay the press-on tape in place on the wrong side of the garment and press in place. Or you can treat the patch edges as you did the darning of tears with corners, running your thread line back and forth over the cut line and making the stitch lines criss cross at the corners.

4. If your fabric is more delicate or loosely woven, baste your patch to thin net or other fabric which is about an inch longer on each side than your patch and hole. In this case the patch is basted first to the net, and then the net is basted to the garment before darning it securely to the edges.

RENEWING COLLARS, CUFFS AND SLEEVES

A shirt or blouse can be worn much longer if you reverse the collar and cuffs when they begin to show wear. Sleeves that are worn along the bottom edge can simply be cut to another length. Many sleeve lengths are popular.

How to Turn a Collar: If this is a standard type of collar on a dress or blouse, it is very simple to take off the collar and finish by reversing it. Simply rip the stitches with a single edge razor

Turning standard type collar

blade. Then turn the collar so that the worn side is on the side that turns under and restitch, after carefully pinning and basting back in place. Restitch it in the same way it was originally sewn.

How to Turn Collar with Neckband: A man's shirt and a woman's tailored shirtwaist would be handled in exactly the same way.

1. Rip out carefully, using a single edge razor blade to cut stitches.

2. Turn collar over, and pin and baste first to the outside of the neckband. Machine stitch.

3. Now pin and baste the other, or inner part of the neckband over the seam you have just stitched. Machine stitch this in place, and press.

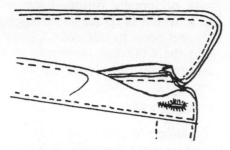

Turning collar with neckband

How to Turn a Cuff: Cuffs are turned exactly the same way as a collar; this means ripping the cuff off with a single edge razor blade, turning over and inserting the sleeve back into the seam and restitching the same way the cuff was made to begin with.

How to Renew Frayed Sleeve Edges: A frayed sleeve edge is a good excuse for rethinking your sleeve length and shortening it to ¾ths or above the elbow length if it will look good on you. However, if the length it is now is the desired length, all you have to do is follow these easy steps.

1. Using your small scissors, clip a thread, and pull out the hem of your sleeve along the seam tape.

2. Press out the crease; turn the hem up a fraction of an inch more so that no frayed edge shows, and pin and press in place. Re-hem.

REPAIRING UNDERGARMENTS

There are all kinds of products on the market to help you add years to your undergarments. There are satin straps, adjustable ones if you prefer, which you can buy to replace the frayed ones you are wearing. There are new elastic backs complete with hooks and eyes so that you can replace that whole segment if the elastic has stretched out of proportion. Or you can simply replace the elastic part, first ripping the seams with a single edge razor.

How to Repair Damaged Lace: There are many ways to repair the lace of your slip or bra. You can lay net underneath the worn lace and hand stitch in place, using tiny overhand stitches to make little ridges like the flowers in the lace, following the original pattern of the lace as much as you can. You can also cut out lace patterns from another piece of lace you have in your mending box, and sew it or glue it over the worn spot. You can buy new lace, and attach a whole new border if you prefer, attaching it to the material of the slip with an overhand stitch or machine stitch, using a zigzag stitch.

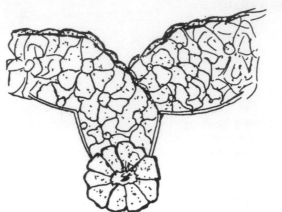

Repairing damaged lace

How to Repair Pulled Out Slip Seams:

1. On the wrong side of the slip, make a new seam on the machine.

2. Holding the two seam allowances together, run a line of zig-zag stitches about a ¼ of an inch from the seam line to act as your seam finish and trim off frayed edge. Press to one side.

3. Turn slip to right side, and top stitch ⅛th inch from seam line being sure to catch the seam allowance underneath.

GLOSSARY OF SEWING TERMS

anchor-stitch, reinforcement stitching back and forth at strategic points for ½ inch or so. Can also be done on machine with zigzag stitch

applique, bits of one fabric used as decoration on another piece of fabric, usually applied with a decorative stitch

armhole, the opening for the sleeve of a garment

arrowhead tack, a triangular embroidered detail used as reinforcement at ends of vents for pockets, pleats and vents in tailored garments

backing, one fabric used to reinforce another fabric

back-stitch, reinforcing the end of a line of stitching by reversing the direction on the machine to restitch on the last few stitches. Also a hand stitch that imitates machine stitching and is used for extra strength

baste-stitch, long temporary stitches used to hold two pieces of material together for final sewing. On the machine set to longest stitch, 6 or 8 per inch. Also used as a pulling thread to ease in caps of sleeves, or as a guiding line for button-holes, center fronts of garments and pockets

belting, a stiff band used to back cloth belts

beveling edges, a method of removing bulk from seams, trimming away the seam allowance inside faced edges, using scissors at slanted angle

bias, any diagonal line in fabric which does not follow the lengthwise or crosswise thread. True bias is the imaginary line which makes a 45 degree angle with the length and width grains and has the most stretch

binding, using a strip of fabric folded over to enclose the edge of another piece of fabric, on both sides

bodkin, a blunt needle used to thread elastic, tape or ribbon through a casing or to turn cording right side out

box plait, the vertical strip on the front of shirts and blouses

canvas, used for interfacing, a firmly woven material, usually cotton or linen

carrier, a loop of fabric or thread used to hold a belt loosely to an area of a garment, such as waistline or hipline

catch-stitch, a crossed hand stitch, used to fasten a raw edge of material to another surface of material, such as in hemming a wool skirt

clean finishing, turning the raw edge of a hem or facing to the inside and stitching along the edge

clip, a short snip made with the point of a scissors into a seam allowance to make garment fit more smoothly. Never cut closer than ⅛th inch to seamline.

cording foot, zipper foot used for stitching zippers and cording on machine, a one pronged sewing machine foot dart, a stitched fold in the garment, which helps it conform to the curves of the human body and which is tapered at one or both ends

directional staystitching, a line of machine stitching in a single layer of fabric used to hold the grain threads in place and prevent stretching. Unless otherwise directed, it is stitched just outside the seamline

directional stitching, sewing seams in the proper direction to hold grain threads in position and prevent stretching or sagging of material

drape, controlling fullness by using pleats, gathers or tucks

drum, a separate lining which is sewn into a skirt but is not sewn into the seams. Helps skirt keep shape

ease, gently working in extra fabric when joining a longer piece of fabric to a shorter one without making gathers or tucks

ease allowance, extra fullness allowed for in a pattern to permit easy movement of the body

edging, Ruffling or lace or other decorative strip of material used for trimming along an edge

edge stitching, topstitching at the edge of such things as collar, cuffs and belts. Also, a row of stitching placed close to a seamline

embroidery, ornamental stitching on cloth, to decorate it, in various designs

emery bag, small pincushion-like bag filled with abrasive powder to remove rust from needles and pins

eyelet, a hand-worked hole or metal ring inserted in a garment for decoration or for holding the prong of a belt buckle

facing, a matching piece of fabric, cut on grain or bias, identical to the garment, used to finish necklines, armholes of sleeveless dresses and other parts of the garment. Sometimes used as decoration to be finished on the right side of garment

fagoting, a decorative stitch for joining two edges. Cannot be used on raw edges

flap, an overlapping piece such as on a pocket opening, to cover the opening

fold, to turn fabric under so that it is double

fray, threads pulled out along the cut edge of material

French tack, a small thread bar—about ½ inch long—attached usually at hem between two parts of a garment, such as coat and lining, to hold them together loosely

frog, a loop fastener usually made of braid or cord, used instead of buttonholes

gathering, rows of stitches drawn up to give fullness.

grading, trimming facings, interfacings and seam allowances after sewing to graduated widths to eliminate bulky seams

grain, the crosswise line and the lengthwise line of the fabric. When these grains lie at perfect right angles the fabric has "perfect grain"

grain line, arrows on paper patterns which indicate the lengthwise grainline the pattern must follow in laying it on the cloth

gusset, extra pieces of material—usually diamond or triangles—inserted into slashes in the material or at the seams to give added fullness, such as under the arms

hemline, the fold line on which the material is turned under to make a hem

hemstitching, a decorative way to finish a hem after threads have been pulled out of the fabric. Also used as embroidery

insertion, (inset) a band of embroidery, lace or other contrasting material used to set into a garment for trimming

interfacing, used to give body, firmness and shape to a tailored garment. It is a layer set in between the garment and the facing

interlining, used to give warmth and help garment hold its shape. It is a layer of fabric inserted between the garment and the lining

lap, the segment of a garment which extends over or covers another segment of the garment, such as in closings of skirts

lapel, the part of the garment below the collar that folds back

layout, the diagram which accompanies every pattern to show exactly how the pieces of the pattern should be pinned to the material for cutting

lining, the extra layer of material sewn inside a garment to help it hold its shape. Usually of a different material than the garment

lockstitching, securing the thread at the beginning and end of the machine stitched row by releasing pressure on the presser foot and stitching back and forth on the same stitch several times

miter, removing the excess fabric from a corner seam allowance by cutting diagonally. Corners are always mitered when two seams cross, in order to make the seam allowance lie flat.

mystik tape, a thin adhesive very useful in sewing that comes in many colors to match the material

nap, the downy or hairy surface of some fabrics, brushed in one direction, as in wool broadcloth, or velvet

needle board, a special pressing board covered with many standing pin points, used for pressing velvets

notches, the little V-shaped or triangular markings along the edge of a pattern to indicate where to match the piece to another, in sewing a seam

notions, (findings) all the little essentials needed to make the garment—buttons, zippers, snap fasteners, tapes, thread, needles and hooks, and trimmings

overcast, long, loose stitches made over the raw edges of seams to keep them from raveling

padding stitches, slanting stitches used to hold interfacings firm and in place in tailoring. Also used in embroidery as the base over which to make satin stitches

picot, an edge finishing for fabric made by cutting through a line of machine hemstitching

piecing, joining pieces of fabric together to extend the material when the pattern is wider than the material, as in a circular or bias skirt

pile, the surface of materials such as velvet and velveteen and corduroy, which have upright surface threads

pinking, a seam finishing of V-shapes or scallops made by cutting along the edge with a pinking shears

placket, the opening in a seam into which zippers and hooks are sewn

pleat, a fold made in the fabric, which adds roominess

preshrink, to pre-wash or steam fabric before cutting so that it will not shrink later after the garment is sewn

quilting, stitching made by machine or by hand through several thickness of material to make designs and hold the layers together

ravel, to pull threads from the edge of the fabric to make a fringe. Also a frayed edge

regulation stitch, (permanent stitch), permanent machine stitching used in sewing most garments—12 to 15 stitches per inch. Fine fabric requires more stitches per inch, heavy fabric, less

revers, lapels on dresses coats and suits, which are folded back to show the reverse side.

rip, to open a seam or row of stitches. Also, to tear material into two parts without using a scissors

rolled hem, a very narrow hem made by rolling the edge of the material between thumb and forefinger and catching with small slip stitches

ruffle, a gathered or pleated strip of fabric used to trim a garment, curtain, etc.

running stitch, the most common hand stitching, running the needle in and out of the material in an even line, with stitches approximately equal distance apart

sag, stretching caused by strain on a garment as in sitting or hanging. Bias cut is especially susceptible to sagging

scallop, a series of half-circle-like curves along an edge, used for decorating or pinking seams

seam, (seamline), the actual line in which two pieces of material are joined together with stitching

seam allowance, the border of fabric beyond the stitch line when a seam is sewed. The seam allowance is indicated on patterns at $5/8$ inch

seam binding, a ribbonlike tape for finishing raw edges

selvage, the narrow lengthwise border running along the edge of fabrics as they are manufactured, the finished edge of fabric

shank, the space between button and garment which allows flexibility and room for the thickness of garment being buttoned. Usually made with thread, but some buttons have their own shank

shirring, several rows of running stitches or machine stitches, drawn tighter through the material to cause fullness

shortstitch, machine stitches, used to reinforce. Usually 18 to 20 stitches per inch

shrinking, steaming, soaking or pressing material before using to contract it to its normal condition before making the garment

sizing, a finish used on yarns and fabrics to give body, strength and firmness

sleeve board, a special small padded ironing board used to press sleeves and sleeve caps without creasing the sleeve

slipstitch, a hand stitch that is made only in the fold of the material so that the stitches do not show on top. A concealed hand stitch

smocking, a decorative stitching which draws the material in gathers to give fullness

staystitch, machine or running hand stitches placed in the seam allowance about $1/8$ inch from the seam line, to prevent the fabric from stretching along the cut edges

steaming, the application of wet heat to remove creases or raise the pile of fabric

stiffening, a fabric used to stiffen parts of the garment—usually crinoline, pellon or horsehair

stiletto, a sharply pointed instrument used to pierce belts or make eyelet holes in garments

straight of goods, the lengthwise grain of the material. However, sometimes also used to refer to the crosswise grain

tack, to fasten two pieces of fabric together loosely, as with bar tack or French tack

tailor's tack, two loose basting stitches joining two pieces of material. When cut apart, they mark pattern directions. Can be used instead of tracing wheel.

top-stitching, a line of stitching sewn on the outside of the garment near the seamline

trace, marking fabric with tailor's chalk or tracing wheel to transfer pattern symbols for directions in sewing. Can also be done by basting.

tracing wheel, a small wheel that can be rolled along the cloth to leave a little row of direction markings

trim, cutting away excess material, especially in the seam allowance after sewing

tuck, a fold that is stitched in place to give shape or fullness to the garment

underlining, a second layer of fabric—usually of the same material as the garment—

cut from the same pattern and used to back the sections of the garment. The fabric sections and matching underlinings are sewn together and treated as one unit during the construction of the garment

understitching, a row of stitching that attaches the facing to the seam allowance so that no stitches show on the outside of garment

unit construction, the technique of assembling sections of a garment to make a unit before attaching it to another section. Each unit is stitched and pressed before joining. This results in less handling of the fabric and a fresher, better looking finished product

vent, a slit or opening at the hem or lower part of a garment

welt, a small applied strip of material used to strengthen seams or to decorate, such as on pocket openings

whipstitch, overhand stitches used to sew two folded edges together

zipper foot, (see cording foot)

INDEX

212

213

NOTES

NOTES

NOTES

NOTES

NOTES

NOTES

NOTES